FORGING AHEAD
FOR GOD

FORGING AHEAD FOR GOD

PERCY WILLS: PIONEER MISSIONARY

DARDA BURKHART

Pleasant Word
A Division of WinePress Group
PW

Pleasant Word (a division of WinePress Publishing, PO Box 428, Enumclaw, WA 98022) functions only as book publisher. As such, the ultimate design, content, editorial accuracy, and views expressed or implied in this work are those of the author.

ISBN 13: 978-1-4141-1365-4
ISBN 10: 1-4141-1365-X
Library of Congress Catalog Card Number: 2008910934

Percy and Margarette Wills.
Photo credit to Horace Draper, Victoria, B.C.

TABLE OF CONTENTS

Foreword

NO ONE PERSON has impacted the west coast of Vancouver Island more than the pioneer missionary the Reverend Percy E. Wills. And no one is more qualified to render inspiring sketches of his illustrious life than his gracious daughter, Darda Jean Burkhart.

Travel Vancouver Island wherever you will—its trails, its logging rails and roads, its beaches, its waterfronts, its penetrating sounds and inlets—and Percy has been there. His name is remembered and revered.

By divine design, the life and service of this stalwart is transported from our collective memory to the pages of this moving biography. Darda captures the essence of Percy's quiet, confident faith, which, like an irresistible magnet, drew men, women and children to the very presence of God.

Right at home in the "rest of faith," Percy welcomed both enormous challenge and crippling adversity with the same alacrity of joy. He would often break forth singing the catching yet beautiful reality, "With Christ in the vessel we can smile at the storm . . . ." Nothing was too small, nothing was too menial, and nothing one might ever ask was ever too much. Such was his servant heart. Humility made the smallest task a sacred privilege, while faith viewed the most formidable task "as good as done."

With an unusual ecumenicity, he was able to look beyond denominational boundaries to the ever-present hand of God. He overlooked the obvious human differences to see the unique reflection of the image of God in His people. Loved by all, he provided strong encouragement and diplomatic skill in the formative stages of several fruitful ministries to the British Columbia coast. His creed: one Lord, one faith, one family.

As a young missionary in 1952, I was blessed beyond measure under Percy's fatherly guidance. Earnest emulation of virtues evident in Percy—faith, hope and love—gave rise to a measure of his gracious demeanor in the life of this young disciple. Like the apostle Paul, he held "no dominion over my faith but was a helper of my joy" (2 Cor. 1:24).

As you traverse these pages, you will find your spirit refreshed and your pace quickened in your walk with God.

—Earl Johnson, Director Emeritus
Esperanza Ministries Association

ACKNOWLEDGMENTS

I COULD NOT have written this book without help for at least two reasons. First, my father, Percy Wills, did not speak of his own accomplishments, which were many, but insisted mainly on telling the wonderful works that God did through others who were with him. In doing so, he led others to embark on an adventure of walking with God and expecting Him to answer their prayers. Second, I was not a part of the mission work on the west coast, and I had never even visited there until Easter weekend of 2008.

I was aided in writing this biography by the books *Splendour from the Sea* by W. Phillip Keller and *Not Without Hope* by Louise Johnson. I am also grateful to Phil Hood for his research file about the Shantymen's Christian Association, which was gleaned from *Men With the Heart of a Viking* by Douglas C. Percy. Hood's file contained a lot of material about the years Percy was on the field. His comment, "Someone ought to write a book about Percy Wills," was my impetus to begin this work. In my late seventies, I had to buy a computer, monitor and printer before I could start this project!

Family members gave me their memories of Percy and Margarette. Friends sent letters sharing their experiences with Percy's work, some of which were sent following his death in 1990. Donnel McLean and three of his sisters, Shirley (McLean) Sutherland, Dorothy McLean and Lois (McLean) Hooks, provided their thoughts about being with Percy at the hospital in Esperanza. Earl Johnson contributed several cogent insights into Percy's character and the gifts he observed while working with him.

The crew of Coastal Missions spent time with me in March 2008 and told me of the help Percy gave them when they began their mission work. Director Roy Getman presented me with an unbelievable treasure: three legal-size files of Percy's writings I didn't know existed! With those papers, I was able to incorporate many of the experiences he had written about, including those during his early days on the Canadian prairies.

Others who gave me help were Joan Van Wyckhouse, who taught me how to use the computer; Linda Hammingh, who reviewed the manuscript; and Jeanne Halsey, who mentored me.

I was privileged that my grandson, Brandon Billester, designed the cover of the book. The back cover photo of me was taken by Carolyn Wing Greenlee.

I want to thank the staff of WinePress Publishing, who were more than helpful in coaching me through this very new world of turning my manuscript into this book.

—Darda Burkhart

INTRODUCTION

WRITING THIS BOOK has been not only a labor of love to honor my parents, Percy and Margarette Wills, but also an assignment from our heavenly Father.

Putting Percy's life story down on paper was first suggested to me after his death. I sent letters to many of the people on his mailing list, informing them of his entrance into glory and asking them to send me memories of their times with him or specific instances they had experienced in his ministry. Several people replied, and I have kept their letters. But the timing was not right for the project. I needed insights from those who worked with him and others who knew him well.

In 2005, my husband and I moved up to the Pacific Northwest to be near my son and his family. After my husband's death, I joined a writing class taught by author Jeanne Halsey, a wonderful teacher and a godly woman. One day after class, she asked me, "Have you ever thought of writing a book?" The question took me by surprise. I replied, "No, I haven't."

But the question nagged at me. What would I write about? I didn't consider myself a writer, and I wondered what prompted

Jeanne to ask me that question. Later, she told me that God had put that thought in her mind, and she had just blurted it out. Not long after that, I was reconnected with Earl Johnson, the director emeritus of the work at Esperanza on the west coast of Vancouver Island. I started the work in the knowledge that God was behind it and would give me the ideas for its production. He would also put me in touch with people who could "fill in the blanks" about Percy's life away from home.

I pray that this record of Percy's work on Vancouver Island and Margarette's unfailing support at home will encourage readers to put their implicit faith in a gracious, loving God who still responds to the heart cries of His beloved children. He will not and cannot fail. He will meet every need, and He still works miracles today for those who decide to believe His Word.

A Tribute to Percy E. Wills

P ERCY WILLS WAS a man who became a "man's man," a "man for all seasons," and a servant to all he met. He did not achieve all these graces easily or quickly. He did not begin as that kind of man, but once he met God, he started on a journey to know Him and to fashion his life according to God's Word. He walked in the supernatural grace of God.

In the words of the old hymn "Amazing Grace," he pursued God "through many dangers, toils and snares." No test was too hard, no trail too long or trial too wearying—they served only to strengthen his faith. He often said he did not have great faith; he had faith in a great God.

Along with the rigors of Percy's daily missionary travel were the care and support of his wife, Margarette, and their children, Frank and me. He daily committed us to God's providential care, whether he was on the field or at home, and prayed earnestly for our continuing growth in the Spirit of God. He kept close watch on our health and educational progress, speaking a few words of godly advice to us as the occasion warranted.

He was also a visionary who saw the needs on the west coast of Vancouver Island. At the same time, he knew that God had the means to meet those needs. With the approval of the local mission board, and backed by the weekly prayer meeting, he stepped out to be the hands, feet and heart of his loving heavenly Father. Through his strong faith in God's leading, he set about to start the process of securing land and materials to build the various mission entities that would serve those unmet needs. Neither ethnic, religious, political nor age classifications had any meaning to him. Anyone who was isolated and without spiritual hope was to be shown the love of God. God did meet those needs time and time again, often at the last moment.

From his experiences, he came to believe that there were three things the Lord asks believers to do: first, to see the invisible; second, to believe the incredible; and third, to do the impossible.

God trained him and perfected him until he was a man in whom all the fruits of the Spirit were visible. He was disciplined and close to the heart of God, and his face shone with that benevolent and attractive Spirit of the living God. When people encountered him, they knew they were in the presence of a man of God and were touched by it.

—Darda Burkhart

CHAPTER ONE

THE LETTER

Your ears shall hear a word behind you, saying, "This is the way,
walk in it," whenever you turn to the right hand or
whenever you turn to the left.
(Isaiah 30:21)

PERCY AND MARGARETTE Wills were the pastors of a successful church in Auburn, Washington. Their family of four included their son, Frank, and me, their baby daughter. They sensed a change was coming in their ministry and had been praying that God would give them direction. They didn't know how or where that change would come or what it would be; they only knew it would come.

Night after night, they sat at their kitchen table and talked about the various issues confronting them. Percy had been approached about going into some kind of evangelistic work, but that did not seem feasible at that time. Adding to their quandary was the fact that Percy's Canadian citizenship was causing a problem for them. He would not be able to stay in the United States indefinitely. (Margarette was an American citizen, born in Oklahoma.)

Margarette's health was also of grave concern. During her pregnancy with me, the doctor had ordered her to bed to reduce the stress on her heart, hoping that she would be able to carry me to term. Grandmother Gardiner and her daughter Millie had come to Auburn to manage the household duties. Millie was only six months older than Frank, and the two of them became inseparable and happily went to school together. The family and the church people prayed earnestly for us. With loving care, Margarette came through, and I was born in May. God had taken care of us both. Margarette later said that she wished she could have had more children, but that was not possible.

During Margarette's pregnancy, as we needed money, I went to work on a potato farm nearby. The labor was difficult, but I was promoted to head of the sorters. When the job was finished, I had earned five dollars, for which we were devoutly thankful; but before I reached home, the Lord sent a man with a fifty-dollar check.

(Percy Wills)

In Margarette's weakened condition after my birth, traveling with a new baby would have

Left to right: Percy, Frank and Margarette Wills holding baby Darda

been very difficult, even dangerous. Then in early June 1930, a letter arrived that seemed to hold the answer to their prayers. The proposal it contained, if accepted, would test their faith in God to undreamed lengths. It would set the course of their lives in uncharted waters, where only God could keep them afloat.

The letter they opened was an invitation for Percy to join the Shantymen's Christian Association (SCA) as a missionary on the west coast of Vancouver Island, British Columbia. The mission headquarters was in Toronto, Ontario, 3,000 miles away. The association had missionaries in the northern parts of the Prairie Provinces and in eastern Canada, but they had no missionary in the western sector.

Percy had been born in Victoria, British Columbia, into a family with roots on the island. His father and mother had settled in Victoria in 1890. In a sense, if they accepted the call, he would be going home.

The move would solve their problem of citizenship, and it would also give Margarette and the children a home with her family while he was traveling. However, the invitation posed problems of its own kind, for it was a change of gigantic proportions. Percy would be away from the family for weeks at a time, and then come home for a few days before returning to his work. Instead of pastoring a successful church as he had been doing, he would be ministering one-on-one with isolated people who had almost no spiritual help available to them. A further consideration was that he would be "living by faith"; that is, he would receive no regular salary but would rely on God to supply the needs for his work and their support. (An early record reports that the salary of a missionary couple was 12 dollars a month—and that only after the mission paid all of its outstanding debts.)

Despite these obstacles, as Percy and Margarette prayed and read and reread the letter, they began to believe that God was pointing the way for them to serve Him in this very different and difficult calling. It was no easy decision, even though they sensed God was leading them. Questions came thick and fast. *Could they do this? Was this really God's answer to their prayers?* They wondered if God would sustain and provide for them as He had done for Percy before he was married.

"Living by faith," as it was called, meant trusting God to provide every need for the one who was engaged in God's work. It was not a novel way of life for Percy, for he had lived in this manner after his conversion as a new Christian. However, at that time he was responsible only for himself, but now he was responsible for three others as well. Could he really believe and trust that God would meet every single need any of them had in a timely manner?

As they prayed sincerely and considered all of these questions and others that arose, they felt the peace of God descend upon them. They felt that this invitation was of God, and so they decided to take this huge step of faith onto an unknown path. They resigned the pastorate and wrote to the committee in Victoria to accept the call.

There were tearful sighs and heartfelt hugs as Percy and Margarette said goodbye to the people they had grown to love. With everything packed up, the family moved back to Canada, still wondering exactly what was ahead for them.

Going Home

Percy Edmund Wills had been born to Frank H. Wills and Sarah Ann (Porter) Wills in Victoria, British Columbia, Canada, in 1898. He was the fourth and youngest in the family of two sisters, Bessie (Wills) Wilderspin and Amy Wills, and one brother, Archie.

Percy's father had left England in 1880 for the brighter opportunities in Canada. He returned to his native Devonshire, England, five years later, where he met Miss Porter. When he returned to Canada, he heard the call to "go west" and went as far west as possible: Victoria, B.C. His fiancée, Annie (as she was known), and three other young women traveled together from England to Canada. Frank and Annie were wed in Vancouver in 1890, and then settled in Victoria in the home Frank had built for them. (He was a building contractor in the city, and some of the homes he built are still inhabited.)

Percy and his siblings attended Spring Ridge School for their first four years and then moved on to the Central School at the top of a nearby hill. That school had separate sections for the boys and girls marked by an iron railing.

Sundays were spent in the local Methodist church. The family attended morning and evening services, and Sunday School classes took up the afternoons. The church had a choir, and Frank Wills had a good true tenor voice. He loved to sing and was a member of the choir for several decades.

Percy was 16 when World War I broke out. His brother, Archie, joined the army in 1915, and Percy joined him a little later. They were both in the Canadian Field Artillery that was sent to England for further training before being sent to the front lines in France.

Left to right: Percy Wills, Archie Wills

While in England, Percy caught the measles, and the whole camp had to be quarantined. He was sent to the military hospital in Plymouth, England. When he recovered, he and Archie visited relatives who lived nearby. Their cousin was noted for her cooking, and she used to stock them up with Cornish pasties and other goodies before they returned to the cold food in France.

Percy returned from the battlefields of France in World War I feeling disillusioned, discontent and discouraged with what he had seen of man's way of solving problems. He found work for the summer of 1919 as one of a survey crew with the Soldier Civil Reestablishment Service in northern Alberta. He thought that getting away from the city would give him a chance to come to terms with his fears. It didn't work.

Around the World

Percy thought a trip around the world with an Army buddy of his would give him the excitement he desired. He later wrote:

> When saying "good-bye" to the family, there were tears, of course, for we did not know where I was going, or when we would meet again. After the farewells, I started down the long ramp to the steamer and was nearing the ticket-taker when I heard hurried footsteps coming behind. I must confess that there was a lump in my throat, as I groped my way, for my heart was as heavy as lead.
>
> Suddenly, I was seized from behind by a strong pair of arms, whirled around and held tight to my father's breast. The words that came were very precious words, and I shall never forget them as long as I live: "Son, when you get into trouble, wire me quick." Never "if," but "when".
>
> (PW)

Percy and his buddy started out on their worldwide trip looking for adventure, but he made it only as far as Winnipeg, Manitoba.

While in that city, he visited some family friends and was invited to church. Even though he had been brought up in church, for the first time he really heard and understood the gospel of Christ's death on the cross for the forgiveness of his sins and that he could be given eternal life as a child of God. When he decided to turn his life over to God, the impact of that decision was pronounced. No longer was he disillusioned, discontent or discouraged. He now had a new outlook on life.

One day he read Mark 5:19 (KJV), which says, "Go home to thy friends, and tell them how great things the Lord has done for thee, and has had compassion on thee." It had such an impact on him that he took it as his life's verse. He called off the trip around the world and instead went home and told his family what God had done for him. Then he remembered the people he had worked with in northern Alberta and their lack of spiritual guidance. He wanted those people to have the same sense of God's presence that he had.

He moved north and became an itinerant missionary, determined to trust God to supply every need he had. For Percy, it was a time of testing and proving the truth of God's promise of provision.

Life as an Itinerant Missionary

The first summer was difficult, because he was living hand-to-mouth in a little shack. He walked between farms or lumber camps with a pack on his back, joyously telling everyone he met that God loved them and would forgive their sins.

> One day I started down the trail and the first farm I approached made me welcome. "Why are you walking?" they asked.
>
> "I have no horse," I said. They took me to the barn and presented me with one.
>
> As I approached the next farm bareback on my pony, I was asked, "Where do you keep your saddle? Are you afraid of wearing

it out?" When the kind questioners learned that I had no saddle, they immediately produced one from the tack room, saying, "It's an old one that nobody uses any more."

(From that day on, whether the need was for a horse, a car, a truck, a boat, or a plane, as soon as the workers would rise and start on the journey, transportation would be provided, and not only equipment, but the fuel to keep it going).

(PW)

Yet the day came when Percy had nothing in his cupboard and no money to buy supplies. Winter lay ahead, and he needed warm clothing to survive. He knew God would have to supply this need. Just then, a farmer knocked on his door, asking if he would like to come and work for him. He was short a man on his threshing crew, he said. Percy took this offer as God's means of supply and accepted the man's offer.

In that northern latitude, the summer season was short but with long daylight hours. Farms were measured in hundreds of acres. Harvesting had to be done quickly and every minute utilized. Teams of men fed the ripened sheaves of grain into the maw of the steam-driven threshing machine. Percy was assigned the job of spike pitcher, who fed the machine. The work was very hard, and even though Percy was physically strong, it was back-breaking labor. His muscles were not used to this type of work, and by the end of the fourth day, he was so sore he could barely move. When it rained the next day, the respite enabled him to recoup his strength and hardened his muscles.

For the rest of the summer, he worked eagerly and determinedly at his job. At times the men harvested the crops on into the night, working by the light of straw stacks set ablaze. At all costs, the harvest had to be brought in before the weather changed.

At the end of the summer, Percy collected his pay, which was eight dollars a day. He immediately planned to send away for the warm winter clothing he needed, but just then a salesman came into the camp taking orders for heavy sheepskin-lined coats. Many of the men, including Percy, paid him 45 dollars each for their order. The salesman turned out to be a con man who took off with their money and was never heard from again.

The men were outraged and called the police to investigate. The authorities asked Percy if he, too, had lost money in the scam. "No, he hadn't," he said. His reply was unusual, but he had previously committed himself and all he had to the Lord, so he reasoned that the money he had given was God's money and that if God wanted to take it, that was all right with him. He truly believed that if he took any loss, whether of goods or reputation, with patience and trust God would work it out for him.

God did just that. Some weeks later, on a Saturday night, Percy was preparing his talk for the next day's service when he heard a knock at the door. When he opened it, he saw a man standing there with a bulky parcel addressed to him from a mail-order house. The man said, "This parcel's for you, sir." Percy was surprised and replied that he hadn't ordered anything from that company. But the delivery man put it in his hands and said, "Well, it's addressed to you, so take it!"

Amazed and excited, Percy took the parcel inside, wondering what it could contain. When he tore open the package, he was astounded to find a beautiful warm fur coat. He could not possibly have afforded such an item, nor would he have ordered it. God was true to His promise of provision, and he was extremely grateful.[1]

This was a foundational lesson for him and one upon which he would base his trust for the rest of his life. Every vision he had for the work required faith not only to birth it but also to see it through to completion.

Time and again, when the resources had dwindled and come to an end, God would provide. Time after time, discouraged, disappointed, and blue, God would revive. Often, when humbled by mistakes and made penitent by blunders, God would come in His loving way and show that He never forsakes.

When I dedicated my life to God for home missionary activity, I had ten cents remaining from the disposal of my affairs. On the morning that I was to leave for a distant place, I prayed and asked God for the need to be supplied for train fares and other incidentals. I felt strangely moved to go to the post office, although I had already cleared my new address through the depot. There was a letter, which had been mislaid, and in the letter was a check for one hundred dollars. From that day on, it has been one succession of hand-to-mouth experiences—"but it has proved to be God's hand and my mouth."

(PW)

Many people told Percy he had great faith. "No," he replied, "I just have faith in a great God." But his strong faith in God was a constant example to his fellow Christians of God's unending compassion and care for the needs of His children.

CHAPTER TWO

TWO BECOME ONE

*And the Lord God said, "It is not good that man should be alone; I
will make him a helper comparable to him."*
(Genesis 2:18)

P
ERCY MET HIS future wife in a most unusual way. As a matter of fact, he had decided not to marry because of the type
and location of his missionary endeavor. His income was
certainly not enough to support a wife, nor was the unpopulated
area where he trekked a good place for a woman to be left alone
for days at a time with no neighbors close by to call on for help.
However, God had other plans, which He set into motion in spite
of Percy's reservations.

In the course of Percy's ministry, he held meetings in the city of
Edmonton, Alberta. One evening, he was asked to visit a woman
in the hospital who had fallen from a streetcar and broken her leg
in three places. The next day, he went to her hospital room and
found her in great pain. Her leg was in a heavy cast, suspended in
traction. After a short time, he offered to pray for her and said a
simple prayer, committing her into God's hands.

The immediate reaction was astounding. She began shouting, "I'm healed! I'm healed!" The nurse was alarmed and came quickly to see what the commotion was. The patient told her to remove the cast, because she was healed. The nurse called the doctor, who thought the woman was delirious in her pain. Not so. She continued to demand that the cast be removed, because she was healed.

Nothing else would quiet her, so the doctor removed the cast. The woman immediately got out of her hospital bed, dressed herself and walked out of the building completely healed. The miracle was the talk of the hospital for days.

Percy quietly went on his way, but the next night, the woman and her daughter attended the meeting. When he spoke to them after the service, he did not know that God had arranged the event so he could meet his future wife.

Percy's habit, begun early in his walk with God, was to spend the first part of each day in prayer and Bible study. While engaged in this practice one morning after the woman's healing, God impressed on him that the woman's daughter, Margarette, was to be his wife. He continued praying about it, because to get married meant a complete reversal of his previous decision to remain single.

Margarette's health was a major consideration. While he was physically robust, athletic and full of energy, she was frail and had a weakened heart. Knowing the rigors of the field he had chosen to work in, he questioned the wisdom of asking her to move to such a lonely place. But he persisted in his prayer and put these questions before his heavenly Father.

Once Percy had determined that it was God's will, he went to Margarette's home to visit. He found her sitting at the piano playing some hymns, which she loved to do. Percy sat beside her and asked if she would accompany him to the mission field. She asked, "Do you mean as your pianist?" "No," he replied, "As my wife." She was very surprised, as you can imagine, for she had barely met him and knew almost nothing about him. She told him that she would have to pray about the matter and would let him know.

Percy returned to his backwoods parish and continued his visitation. For three weeks, he heard nothing from Margarette. He was sure that He was acting in God's will, but how would she react? He alternated between hope and despair, not knowing how she would reply. One moment he was elated, thinking of his deep, growing love for her; the next he feared she would reject him. He continued to have questions about how her health would fare on his mission field. All he could do, and did do, was to continually commit their future into the hands of God.

One day, Percy received a telegram saying, "I cannot eat, sleep, or work without thinking of you. My answer is 'yes!'" He was elated about their future together, for his deep loving nature needed someone upon whom to lavish that love. His parish was simply not enough.

Thus, another important part of God's plan for him fell into place. It was certainly not the pairing he would have imagined, or even chosen, had he considered marriage at all. But God had chosen a perfect partner for him, a woman strong in spirit, extremely capable, and in love with him—a love that God had birthed in her heart.

Family History

Margarette had an interesting background. Her grandmother, known to our family only as "Granny" Williams, was the daughter of a local bishop of the Church of England in Wales. She was pledged to marry the nearby landowner (which would have consolidated the two estates), but she did not like the arrangement, for she was in love with the family coachman. The two soon took matters into their own hands and eloped. After their wedding, when she tried to enter her home, her father told her to use the servant's entrance. She was no longer his daughter. She had been disowned.

The couple immigrated to the United States and settled in Oklahoma, near Krebs, and made their home in a sod house. This was Indian Territory at that time, and some of the Indians made friends with them. They would show up at any time of the day for coffee. They came to trust "Granny Williams" and even asked her to act as midwife for the Indian women.

Thirteen children were born into the family. Margarette's mother, Maggie, was the twelfth in the order. Mr. Williams and five of his sons worked in the coal mines. One day, the sound of a terrible explosion was heard in the town. The explosion was in the mine, and it killed all the men who were working down in the shafts. Families were devastated by the loss of their men-folk; there were no social service aids or welfare systems at that time to help them. Granny Williams was left with several children but had no means of support to raise them. She did, however, have a deep faith and trust in God to care for them, which He did. The only means of income open to her was to take in boarders, and this she did.

When Maggie was 15 years old, she married a Scotsman named James Lohoar. He, too, was a coal miner. They had two children, John and Margarette, my mother, who was born in McAlester, Oklahoma.

In about 1907, James moved his family to Alberta, where he became boss of a coal mine. In 1914, he and some friends took one last fishing trip before joining the Army to fight in World War I. When their boat overturned in the deep lake, Grandfather James saved several of his friends who couldn't swim, but then he succumbed to a cramp and lost his life. His eulogy at the funeral included Jesus' words in John 15:13 (KJV): "Greater love hath no man than this, that a man lay down his life for his friends."

His family was grief-stricken. John seemingly never got over his father's death. Immediately, at the age of 14, he felt the responsibility to be the "man of the family." Margarette was then only 10 years old, and the three of them drew much closer in a bond of mutual dependence and love.

Maggie and her children moved to Edmonton to be near her brother, Sam. There, the brother and sister became business partners in a barbershop and beauty parlor. Maggie also opened a bakery to provide for her family. John rigged up a signal system between the two shops to let Maggie know if she was needed in the beauty parlor. It was in that city that Maggie fell from the streetcar and broke her leg and my father, Percy Wills, came to pray for her, resulting in her healing.

Through this long and torturous journey, God brought Percy and Margarette together in a union that lasted almost 50 years. Their marriage was truly "made in heaven" and became an example and blessing to all who were touched in some way by their lives.

CHAPTER THREE

THE FIELD

For we are God's fellow workers; you are
God's field, you are God's building.
(1 Corinthians 3:9)

W HEN GOD PREPARES a person for his or her life's
work, He also prepares the field in which he or she
will work. So it was with Percy and Margarette.
While they were developing their faith during the testings that
God allowed, God was also preparing the mission to which Percy
would be called.

The mission was known as the Shantymen's Christian
Association, presently known as SCA International. It had begun
in Canada in the early 1900s as an itinerant work among the
people in the northern areas of Canada, where the population was
scattered. Men worked in logging, wood mills, the mining industry
or on farms, and most villages were too small to have their own
church and pastor. Men whose hearts were aflame with love for
Jesus trekked on foot or horseback to these places with a Bible,
literature and the message of salvation.

After World War I, the mission, under the leadership of William Henderson, began looking westward to survey the need in the Prairie Provinces and over the Rockies to the area north of Vancouver, British Columbia. For two summers in the early 1920s, Mr. Henderson and party ranged along the mainland coast, visiting the villages and logging camps to give the gospel message to any and all who would listen. Many did come to know the Lord, but the great lack of spiritual guidance was very evident.

According to the book *Men with the Heart of a Viking* by Douglas C. Percy, one man named William Fuller began a work on the Pacific Coast in about 1920. His ship, the *Messenger*, was a former Japanese fishing vessel that had been seized for bootlegging and was converted into a gospel messenger. Fuller and his party traveled up and down the Pacific coast in this boat for about five years, until he moved on to another type of mission work. Unfortunately, we have no record of the results of his work on the coast. The ship was dismantled in 1929.

Another man with a burden for the people soon came on the scene. Known as "Uncle Sammy" Whiting, he was the representative and manager of the Cadbury Fry Company on Vancouver Island. He was a godly man, full of vitality and the love of Christ. As he traveled up and down the island, he saw the great spiritual need of the people who lived on the ranches, farms and in the backwoods. They were almost forgotten by the churches, for access to them was difficult.

Whiting's concern produced an action plan. In Victoria, his home city, he gathered a group of people together whose main purpose was to pray for the souls of those who were on his mind. This group of dedicated Christians, many of whom were elderly and of simple means, met each week for prayer. (These prayer meetings still continue weekly in Victoria after more than 80 years!) Their prayers to God for the work were the major mainstay of support for Percy and Margarette and other workers who later joined the mission.

In 1928, Uncle Sammy contacted the Shantymen's Christian Association about procuring a missionary for the island. The group continued to pray as they awaited word from the mission. One older man undertook the task of visiting some of the ranchers and farmers scattered over the island. Although his spirit was bright and strong, his physical health was not equal to the task.

A couple of years later, someone who had learned of Percy's work in the backwoods of Alberta suggested his name to the local committee. The secretary of the committee was Percy's brother-in-law, Ernest Wilderspin. He was asked to draft a letter to Percy asking him to become their missionary to the people on Vancouver Island. It was this letter in June 1930 that changed the course of Percy and Margarette's lives. In God's timing, the field of service had now been prepared for the couple whose training in faith and service was ready to meet the need.

> My call was especially apparent on the "Graveyard [of the Pacific]." The two or three missionaries who worked there were hampered by lack of interest and equipment. Hundreds of thousands of dollars have been spent by missionary societies on marine activity on the West Coast of the British Columbia mainland, and "inside" [coast of] Vancouver Island, but on the outside [coast] where the need of medical and spiritual attention was far greater, the interest lagged—or rather, did not exist.
>
> (PW)

Into a Difficult Field

The mission field to which Percy and Margarette were invited was the harsh and inhospitable west coast of Vancouver Island. It was as rugged and isolated as almost any other part of the world. The only roads were unpaved logging roads, and none of the roads connected one bay to another. Evergreen trees grew all over the hills and mountains, even down to the water's edge. The mountains themselves plunged into the depths of the ocean, and ships were at danger from rocks and reefs when they entered the inlets. There were few large areas of relatively flat land along the coast where large communities could be built. People lived in small huts at the head of a bay or along the water in a protected spot away from the ocean surge. For centuries, the native people—who were later known as "First Nations" people—had located themselves at the heads of the inlets in settlements both large and small.

> Among the people of our "hinterland," a man may travel across its difficult trails, may wander beside its marvelous lakes, or gaze upon the grandeur of its scenery, and come to a lonely hut or shack, and find therein the same human problems, the same heartaches, the same joys, the same sorrows as in the more civilized population.
>
> (PW)

The west coast of Vancouver Island has been nicknamed the "Graveyard of the Pacific" for good reason. For most of the length of the coast, there is no protective island or landmass to break the oncoming combers that roll across the ocean. When lashed by the howling winds of a winter storm, waves crash against the rocky shoreline, their crests blown into drenching, battering spray.

> The Pacific Ocean sweeps in from the west, and its tides run in and out around Cape Scott on the west and Cape Flattery to the southeast. From Cape Flattery, the sea runs in the Straits of Juan De Fuca through the Gulf of Georgia to meet the tides coming in the opposite direction from Cape Scott. The latter tides sweep down from the west past Bull Harbor and into Johnstone Straits, where many difficult tide rips form, as well as a few whirlpools.

Bucking these tides is impossible except by the fastest boats. Most ships wait for favorable tides to run such passages as the Seymour Narrows.

(PW)

Every year ships are blown onto the rocks by the wicked, stormy winds of winter, only to be battered into debris by the incessant waves acting like jackhammers. Incautious, foolhardy men trying to beat an oncoming storm have been lost at sea, their bodies never recovered. Added to this danger is the impact of the weather for a large part of the year. Daylight hours shorten during the fall and winter, when rain sometimes lasts for days. Rainfall in some areas is measured in feet, not inches. Gray clouds hang low, often blocking out the sun for days. The sound of rain dripping off the trees, the mournful cry of the seagulls, and the smell of salt spray on rotting leaves can lead one to a state of depression.

In the early years during the winter, life was difficult. Some people did not leave their cabins for days unless it was necessary. It was hard for children who wanted to play outside, because much of the area was muddy. When they came back indoors, their footprints marked the floors, which then had to be mopped. If there was no electricity in the cabin, wet laundry hung inside, adding another element to the dampness. Late spring and summer, however, brought beautiful days when the sun rose early and set quite late. The wind slowed to a breeze, and things started to dry out. People with "cabin fever" came out to visit neighbors; children ran around and played. Life took on a happier mien.

In the early days of the mission work, about 4,000 people lived along the coastline. Whites, First Nations people and Japanese made up the population. The men worked at the mining and logging camps, wood mills and canneries.

In the contact of everyday life, the Shantymen have found their greatest outlet for the ministry. In lighthouses, on the trail, in the camps and fishing villages, reserves are dissipated and the intimate contacts are made. Many a service has been held in beer parlors, blacksmith shops, schoolhouses, and homes. One of the best remembered of all was on the shores of Useless Inlet. Only four men were present but it was one hundred percent of the population. The meeting was held on the seashore around a campfire, with a drizzle of rain falling over all; but had a bishop or an archbishop been present, the Spirit of God could not have been more real or precious.

(PW)

The Whites and the First Nations people kept themselves apart. The "white man" had exploited the natives for years, and distrust had built up between them. The white people considered the natives to be illiterate pagans. In addition to this division, the Canadian government had enacted a policy of assimilation and founded residential schools for the First Nations children. Many were "taken from their families, stripped of clothes and of identity [and] forced to stay in a strange place with no mother, father or grandparent to comfort them." Dr. Bobby Joseph, a First Nations chief, later recalled, "I remember feeling hauntingly lonely starting at age six, and a long time later I'd feel it again when something triggered it."[1]

Getting to Know Neighbors

When Percy began visiting the families on the coast, he treated both the Whites and the First Nations people equally. After a while, the natives began to realize that this white man was not going to misuse them for his own purposes. He cared for them, loved them as they were, sang and told Bible stories to their children, and comforted them in their troubles. He shared donated clothing with them as well. No other person had treated them as if they were worthy of care, and it had a telling effect on them.

Percy is credited with helping the First Nations people, the white people and the coastal folk live and work together in harmony. I was privileged to hear recently one of the First Nations men say publicly that the considerate care of Percy Wills and Dr. McLean was the reason he could stand as a Christian man and preach the gospel. I believe that is rare praise.

While walking the trail one day, I was concerned about the need of a building in one of the districts further up the coast. Costs, as well as labor and materials, were uppermost in my mind. Suddenly I blurted out as though I was addressing an unseen listener, "But we haven't any money. We just can't tackle it now!"

As though Someone were walking the trail with me, I heard a voice saying, "Will you call Me a liar? I have never asked you to do anything for which I have not made Myself responsible!" Thus it has always been from the beginning of my trail. We may not call God a liar with impunity. When He asks us to do anything He immediately makes Himself responsible for the provision of the things and persons, as the need becomes apparent.

[One time] I was conducting meetings in a frontier town and had rented a hall in the center of the village. During the opening meeting, a number of fellows congregated in the rear of the building and commenced making a disturbance. Suddenly, calling the meeting to order, I made my way down to the back of the hall and confronted the men who were making the noise. Picking out the ringleader of the group, I said, "Son, do you know that God loves you?" Immediately there was an uproar from the rest of the gang.

Again I pressed the question on the leader, who was becoming more and more uneasy. Each time the question was pressed home, the gang laughed, but each time it was less uproarious. Gradually a hush came over the whole meeting and I cried once more, "For God SO loved . . ."

Suddenly a sob broke from the leader of the gang, and he cried, "Stop! Is it possible that He could love me?"

There was another disturbance that night as several of those men came forward to the altar and confessed Christ as their Savior. The leader became a powerful force for the Lord as he proclaimed Christ to his mates throughout the downtown district. God's words, jet-propelled by the Spirit of God, touch the core of every problem.

(PW)

God had also prepared Percy for this rugged mission field in another way. Percy's mother, Sarah Ann Porter, was from Devonshire, England. She had come from a long line of Royal Navy personnel, some of whom had sailed with Sir Francis Drake in the late 1500s. All of her brothers were in the Royal Navy. Percy seems to have inherited this call of the sea, for he loved the ocean even when it was angry and turbulent.

I don't know when he learned his seamanship or who trained him in ship handling, chart reading and all the other things necessary to pilot a ship on the dangerous west coast of Vancouver Island, but I do know that God kept him safe through many years of sailing in both the *Messenger II* and *Messenger III*. He was also instrumental in the construction of both ships. His father, Frank Wills, was a highly experienced building contractor, and maybe this skill was passed on to Percy as well.

CHAPTER FOUR

THEIR MISSION BEGINS

*Two are better than one, because they have a good reward for their
labor. For if they fall, one will lift up his companion.*
(Ecclesiastes 4:9-10)

PERCY AND MARGARETTE were married in Edmonton
in May of 1922. She was 19, and he was 24. It was truly
a marriage made in heaven, although the pairing seemed
strange to some.

Percy was active and physically strong, while she was hampered
by thyroid and heart problems. However, though her physical state
was weak, she had a strong spirit and was a very capable woman. He
was called by God to serve isolated people with the gospel, while
she stayed home and worked as a secretary to provide some of the
family income. They were united in their love and commitment
to God and His will, as well as to each other. That commitment
remained steady through the next 50 years of their marriage until
Margarette's death in 1972.

Percy left the North Country to go to Edmonton for his wedding
with 15 dollars in his pocket, which his parishioners had given

him along with their best wishes. He expected the sum would be sufficient to buy the ring and pay for the marriage license and the minister, but when he arrived in the city, he discovered that 15 dollars would not cover his requirements. The license cost $7.50, the ring cost $8.50 (including the inscription) and, on top of that, the minister's wife told him he needed a new suit! The one he was wearing was just not acceptable. After all, he was marrying one of the finest young women in Edmonton. The wedding would not be a simple family affair in the home as he had thought, but would be held in the church decorated with beautiful flowers. Hundreds of guests had been invited to witness the event.

Percy went back to his room that night, penniless and in great distress. He knew that his resources were gone and that no other money was available. As was his custom, he went to the only source he knew: his God. He spent the night in prayer asking God to supply this immediate, overwhelming need. He rose from his knees with peace in his heart, sure that God would provide.

The next day, he met Margarette to go shopping. When they left the house, the postman approached and asked if a Percy Wills lived there. When he identified himself, the postman handed him two envelopes. One was marked "O.H.M.S." (On His Majesty's Service) and contained an official government check for 100 dollars, a large sum in those days. The other envelope was from his family in Victoria and included a check for 25 dollars as their wedding gift.[1]

Percy's heart leaped with praises to God for this prompt answer to prayer. It was also an encouragement to Margarette to see how faithful God would be in supplying their needs. Many times over the course of their marriage they would find God faithful in similar ways. The necessary provision would always come on time—often at the last moment.

With money in hand, the couple proceeded happily to town to complete their shopping. Percy bought a new suit and paid for the ring and the engraving. The flowers were ordered, and gifts were purchased for the wedding attendants. Altogether, they felt the day's shopping was most successful.

That evening, the wedding ceremony took place at the church. Congratulations were extended and gifts were received. One of them was a beautiful hand-painted cup and saucer that I still use on special occasions.

Their First Home

Mr. and Mrs. Percy E. Wills went back to their new abode in northern Saskatchewan, where they were given a room in an old farmhouse as a honeymoon retreat. Percy had worked hard painting and wallpapering it to be ready for their return. Unfortunately, that first night they found that "critters" in the form of bedbugs had already moved in.

Margarette had no trouble sleeping, but Percy couldn't stop squirming. Finally, he got up and said to her, "You light the lamp while I swat them!" While the bugs had feasted on him, they had totally ignored her. It seems that she was immune to insect bites, for even years later she never got bitten by mosquitoes. Since they couldn't use the room, the couple pitched a small tent in a grove of trees on the property and stayed there for the next few days before resuming their work in the town.

The new couple soon began pastoring a small church in town, even though Percy had no Bible School or seminary training. Some of the older men in the congregation were well versed in the Scripture, which made him feel inadequate to minister properly to them. He was troubled about this and prayed earnestly that God would show him how to present the gospel to them.

His answer came one day while he was praying: He would preach only about Jesus and the work He had done for them. He would speak about God's love, grace and provision for all of one's life. When he focused on the ministry of Jesus, the church began to grow in numbers and spiritual depth.

God's Amazing Power

Percy arranged to hold some tent meetings on a farm a short distance from town. Word spread quickly from farm to farm that the meetings had been planned, and people soon began to arrive, some from distant areas. Families set up small tents so they could stay a few days, enjoy the camaraderie, and hear the gospel message.

In response to the preaching of the Word, the presence of God came down in power. Many people, young and old alike, were convicted of their sin and saved. They rejoiced in their new life in Christ Jesus, and there was great joy and fellowship among the 80 to 100 families attending the camp meeting. This supernatural presence of God became evident in Percy's life from that time until his life finished its course.

Local farmers, seeing the need, gave generously of food and other supplies to provide for those in attendance, who generally did not have ready cash. One night, the cook, a new Christian, confided to Percy there was no bread for breakfast, nor was there any place near town to buy enough. The two men knelt and prayed that God would somehow provide. And God did—miraculously.

The next morning when the cook went to prepare the meal, he found loaves and loaves of fresh-baked bread on the table, more than enough to feed the crowd. There was no other explanation for this supply than God's provision. The people were told of this miraculous event, and everyone said grace with grateful hearts.[2] I think it was probably the best bread they had ever eaten.

Starting a Family

Not long after these meetings, Margarette discovered that she was pregnant. Because of her heart trouble, it would be a high-risk pregnancy, so Percy resigned from the little church and took a pastorate in Edmonton in order to give her access to the medical care she needed. His salary was 25 dollars a week, which was not quite sufficient for their needs at that time. However, in His faithfulness, God continued to provide for them, even though at times it was at the last minute.

In 1923, Margarette delivered a healthy baby boy, Francis Howard Edmund Wills, my brother. The couple thanked God with grateful hearts for this new blessing, but the doctors warned them that she must not have any more children, for to do so would risk her life as well as the baby's. They told her that her heart was not strong enough to stand the rigors of another pregnancy.

During that year, Percy began pastoring a small church in Calgary. The couple rented a one-room apartment in a home owned by the Coulter family. The four girls in the family were about the same age as Margarette, and they often helped baby sit Frank. The whole family became fast friends with Margarette and Percy, and their friendship lasted throughout their lives.

One of the members of that church remarked on Percy's steadfast trust in God's provision. One day she visited Percy and Margarette in their home at the Coulter's. While she was there Percy said happily, "See how well God supplies our needs." He opened the cupboard door to show her the food they had on hand. They knew their great Provider was caring for them.

On some occasions, Percy admitted that there were times when they were tempted to feel that the Lord needed their help in providing the necessary items for daily living. One such occasion was at Christmas time in 1925. As Percy relates:

> We were without food in our home and Christmas was just a few days away. We prayed most earnestly until the 21st of December. Then we told the Lord that we were going out to earn the money for our children's festivity. Snow came, and after two terrible

days of shoveling wet, heavy snow from the streets into a leaky truck, we had earned four dollars; but before you could say, "Jack Robinson," the Lord sent in another twelve.

(PW)

Left to right: Frank Wills, Margarette and Percy Wills.
Millie Gardiner in back left, bent over.

I do not know exactly when Margarette and Percy moved back to Edmonton, but when they did they shared a home with her widowed mother, Grandmother Gardiner. Percy left the ministry and took a job in an advertising or insurance agency so that they would have a regular salary. Margarette also got a job working with Grandmother at the Great West Garment Factory. Among my keepsakes is a handwritten letter, dated February 20, 1927, from Percy to his father in Victoria. In this letter, he refers to having a lot of correspondence "at the office where one learns speed instead of efficiency, and you get tired of pen and ink and paper."

During this period, Percy's once-vital spiritual life was put on hold. In his later years, he told me that he had backslidden. What turned him back wholeheartedly to God was an incident concerning his little son's health.

When Frank was about four years old, he and his aunt Mildred, who was only six months older than him, were playing at Grandmother's house. All the adults were at work, and a cleaning lady was doing the floors. She put the two children out on the porch to play and would not let them come back in the house. They got chilled in the bitter cold of winter, and Mildred, in an attempt to keep Frank warm, gave him her shirt. They were hungry, but the only thing they had to eat was an orange the cleaning lady had given to them. They ate even the peel.

In spite of the children's distress, the woman would not let them come back in on her clean floors. Only when Margarette and Grandmother returned from work late in the day were they scooped up and taken at once into the warmth. Both women were irate, and they fired the woman on the spot, telling her never to come back. Fearful for the little ones' condition, they did everything they could to bring color and warmth back into the two small bodies.

Because of this exposure, Frank became ill with infantile paralysis, now known as polio. At that time there were no vaccines or medications to prevent this disease, and doctors were helpless to combat it. Margarette, Percy and Grandmother were heartsick as they watched their beloved son lying inert in his bed. He did not respond to their loving ministrations, and nothing seemed to bring him any relief.

In desperation, Percy prayed to God and vowed to serve Him unreservedly if He would heal Frank. In that prayer, he also stipulated that God would have to care for his family while he was away from them. Shortly thereafter, Frank began to stir and respond. Within hours he was sitting up on his grandmother's lap, laughing and playing.

Since God had kept His part of the bargain, Percy kept his. He resigned his position at the agency, where he had done well, and went back into the ministry. In 1928, he was called to pastor a church in Auburn, Washington.

Percy and Margarette formed loving bonds of Christian fellowship with the people in the congregation. When the church decided to build, God provided the means. One lady, a Mrs. Mosher, gave the property. One of the men in the congregation, John Stewart, brought his tractor and bulldozed and graded the land. His brother, James Stewart, and other volunteers joined Percy in doing much of the construction. When the church was completed, it was named Full Gospel Church.

A lifelong friendship soon formed between the Wills family and the two Stewart families, who were noted for their genial hospitality. After we left Auburn, whenever we were in the area and visited the families, we were always warmly welcomed. To this day, I am in frequent contact with one of the grandchildren in the family.

A New Commitment

In 1930, the letter from the Shantymen's Christian Association arrived and forever changed the direction of Percy and Margarette's lives. They believed it was God's leading and stepped out to follow it.

Percy's mission assignment was a pioneer one. There was no proper housing or schooling available for his family on the west coast of the island, which was then a very primitive area. Margarette's health was still an issue, and Percy did not want her to be left alone with two small children while he was away for weeks at a time. So, the family moved in with Grandmother once again. In addition to Grandmother, Margarette, Frank and me, the family now consisted of Aunt Mildred, a foster girl named Hazel, Uncle John and "Uncle Charlie," Grandmother's permanent boarder. When Percy came home for a short time, there were nine people in the house. If Uncle John went away on a job for a while, Grandmother would often take in another boarder.

This happy arrangement lasted throughout the Depression years. I do not recall ever being hungry or lacking any basic provision during this time. Everyone in our neighborhood was in a similar circumstance, so we never thought of ourselves as "poor." I do, however, recall how I seemed to catch every cold or childhood disease that went around. When any of us got measles, mumps or chickenpox, the doctor or health department representative would come by and put a red card on the door, stating that the house was quarantined. I think the adults were allowed to go to work, but the children could not go to school until the contagious period was over. Inoculations for these diseases came many years later.

Another instance of my parents' trust in God for us children happened when I was about seven or eight years old. I was very thin for my age, and my parents were concerned about my health. Margarette asked a visiting minister who prayed for the sick to come to our home and pray for me. He arrived and talked to us, and then prayed that God would "put meat on my bones." God answered that prayer and I began to thrive, especially after we moved to Victoria. My health has been quite good and my weight stable ever since. I am truly blessed that my parents brought that minister to pray for me and trusted that God would answer their request.

One summer while Percy was home for a short while, he took our family to White Rock, located right on the border with the United States, where Uncle John had reserved a cottage for a few days. As we drove there in our family's Model A Ford, Percy got us all singing. We sang choruses and the old song, "Daisy, Daisy, give me your answer, do," and even some ditties that Percy made up. He was good with children and knew how to keep us occupied on long car trips. We never asked, "How long before we get there?"

Margarette was an excellent secretary with years of experience in Edmonton, before and after her marriage. Although jobs were scarce, she was hired by an insurance agency. She went to work every day, even though at times the walk of two blocks from the streetcar stop to the house taxed her energy. She would often arrive at the door out of breath and panting. Each day, however, she trusted God to give her the strength to get through that day. On weekends, she rested up for the next week's labors.

Another letter among my keepsakes was written by Margarette to Percy sometime in 1938. She writes, "So glad to get your letter and to know you are OK. I slipped on the oiled floor tonight and wrenched my heart—boy I feel sick. Guess it will pass off if I rest up tonight . . . my nerves are shot tonight so I am not going to write much."

After coming home from work, Margarette and Grandmother would sit and embroider or crochet while we all listened to the radio. Since I was the youngest, I was put to bed first. The older children stayed up and did their homework until it was their bedtime.

When the family was settled in Vancouver, Percy began his ministry "on foot and with a pack on his back," as he sometimes said. He later wrote, "I joined this society in 1930, arriving in Victoria with ten cents in my pocket and a pack on my back. From that day till this God has been more than faithful, daily loading us with benefits. I have too often treated God like a penny-pinching miser. If I ask God for peanuts, I get peanuts; but when I treat him like the great God that he is, he acts like the King of kings. As the old hymn suggests, 'Large petitions with thee bring, thou art coming to a King.'"[3]*

Percy hiked the trails of Vancouver Island and visited with families to get acquainted. The trails were mere footpaths and not well kept up, and they were often overgrown with bushes and tree roots ready to catch the toe of a boot. The trees overhead, while providing some protection from the frequent rains, dripped water constantly. Percy owned a hand-knitted Indian sweater made from unwashed wool

*This excerpt was taken from *Decision* magazine, June 1976; Billy Graham Evangelistic Association; used by permission, all rights reserved.

that was virtually waterproof. The one drawback was the pervasive, unpleasant smell of wet wool. Yet so convinced was he of God's will in this venture that he doggedly persisted in visiting the isolated homes, whether they held one person, a couple or a family.

A Written Record

Percy had a gift for writing. As he plodded along a trail, his busy mind crafted poems. As he surveyed his surroundings, he thought of God's greatness and His presence. He meditated on the Scriptures and put his thoughts down on paper. He continued writing all through his life and left a gift of many poems and short sayings.

In 1933, he published a collection of his poems titled *Rambling Rhymes from the Graveyard*. The proceeds from the sale of his booklet went to his mission work. (I was greatly surprised and delighted a few days ago when one of these booklets was found and given to me.) His great concern was to reach everyone he could to communicate the same love of Jesus to them that he had experienced. He wanted the love of God to be evident in every part of his life and did not want anything he did to impede that communication.

Margarette with Percy Wills wearing his Indian sweater

One of his decisions was that he would never introduce himself by using a denominational label. He believed that such a declaration would put up an immediate barrier between him and those he visited. For this reason, he declined to join any particular church, even though he was welcome in any congregation. His main purpose, he believed, was to tell people about the love of Jesus Christ—that He died on the cross so their sins could be forgiven and they could have a new life of joy and peace. He constantly demonstrated that joy and peace in his own life.

Whenever Percy saw that a family needed help, he did what he could to help them. If they were working a small farm, he would pitch in and help with the chores. The warmth of his personality and his love for God made him quickly seem like one of the family. He told the children Bible stories to acquaint them with Jesus, and before he left, he would give the family some Christian literature and pray with them. Later, when he was on the boat, he would give out boxes of clothing.

The trails often led to logging and mining camps, where the men eyed Percy to see if he had the physique their type of work required. Had Percy not spent years in the northern prairies getting inured to the rigors of working on farms and hiking long distances, he never would have earned the opportunity to witness in these camps. He arm wrestled the men and won, demonstrating his strength. Once the men knew he could work as they did, they came to the meetings in the dining hall. Some responded to his message and were saved, but many were not touched. These men were hardened by life away from civilization, families and godly influences. Yet it was Percy's desire that they, too, should hear the gospel as long as he had the opportunity to be there.

An old fisherman said to the Shantyman one day, "If you guys are going to bring missionaries up on this Coast, don't bring fellows who only know how to preach sermons. Get men who know how to cut hair, or mend shoes, or do a job, as well as preach." This was crystallizing what had already become apparent in the work.

(PW)

I often wondered what Percy ate and where he slept when he hiked along these trails. I'm told that when he visited a family, he would often be invited to eat with them. When he was in the camps, he would eat there and sleep in the bunkhouse. On the trails he took many hardboiled eggs with him, because they were nutritious, lightweight and easy to carry.

Some of the abodes that Percy visited were often primitive shacks built with whatever materials were at hand. This made for some humorous incidents. One time, a lady was so happy to have a visitor that she made some tea for Percy. When she offered it to him, he noted that it was her only cup, so he decided to hold it in his left hand and drink from that side. The lady watched him intently, and then said, "My, my, you're left-handed, too." Another time, he visited an old man living alone with his dog. When the man ate his meal, he would leave some of it for the dog, which would then lick the plate clean. He may not have washed his dishes after every meal.

I'm sure that Percy prayed quietly before sipping his tea or eating from plates in such homes. But I never heard of him catching any diseases from the unwashed dishes. In all things, he trusted completely in God for the care of his physical well-being.

CHAPTER FIVE

LOOKING OUT TO SEA

Enlarge the place of your tent, and let them stretch out the curtains
of your dwellings; do not spare; lengthen your cords
and strengthen your stakes.
(Isaiah 54:2)

THE VISION OF the Shantymen's Christian Association was taking the gospel to people who lived far from churches and population centers. Missionaries made the circuit of the area assigned to them by walking or on horseback.

It did not take long for Percy to realize that while the association's vision was good for the interior of the Canadian continent, it was not applicable to the west coast of Vancouver Island. Most of his mission field could not be accessed except by logging roads. Only a boat would serve to transport him from one inlet or bay to the next where people could be visited.

God had trained Percy well over the years for this assignment, and Percy had learned to trust in Him for every provision. The work he had done on farms and the long hikes he had taken to reach people had enhanced his muscular frame. He met and witnessed to different kinds of people, and the opposition and setbacks he often endured instilled a courage and doggedness in him to continue until God's purpose was completed. The church organization he had learned in his several pastorates would be helpful as the number of believers in the villages grew and churches were formed. He would need all of these capabilities and more to establish a spiritual beachhead in the territory he entered that was held in the darkness of sin and ignorance of the gospel.

Percy began his mission survey of the west coast of Vancouver Island in the summer of 1932, taking a canoe trip to assess the area of his new field of service. Immediately he saw the spiritual need of the people who had no church, no medical help and no hope. In their isolation, mothers died in childbirth, men injured by machinery had no emergency care, and others succumbed to chronic illness and died. There was no pastor to conduct funerals. Families did all they could to bury their loved ones, but grieved that they could not provide a better resting place or have the services of a minister to conduct the burial.

Even if an injury could be attended to, the weather often made it impossible for a boat or float plane to land and transport the person to the nearest medical office. Often the closest medical help was Victoria, or even Vancouver, depending on the severity of the injury.

Surveying the Coastline

The west coast of Vancouver Island was not only a rugged area but also a most dangerous coastline. The Olympic Peninsula of Washington State sheltered only the lower part of Vancouver Island; the longer northern part was open to the Pacific Ocean.

There was no landmass between Japan and the west coast to deflect the powerful waves that rolled eastward and smashed against the shores during winter storms. It was aptly named "The

Graveyard of the Pacific," for both large freighters and smaller boats were broken in pieces during heavy storms, leaving their debris to litter the edge of the water.

Percy rented an Indian canoe with two sets of oars for his first survey. The canoe's complement included Percy, Alex Richardson (a friend from Sooke) and a young guide, Philip Mack. The men made Ucluelet their base and started out to survey Barkley Sound. They visited the small settlements during the day, and then camped under a tarp at night. They told everyone they met about the good news of salvation.

When Percy returned the canoe to the owner at the end of the summer, he had no money to pay the rental. What he did have was a very good sheath knife, which he offered to give in exchange for the rental. His offer was accepted, and that was how the bill was paid.

The men were encouraged with the success of their summer's work, and Percy felt that God's call to this mission area was confirmed. He made plans for the following summer with the knowledge that God would have to provide the money for him to return to this field. Their treasury was now empty, but God had proved faithful in the past, and Percy expected He would do so again. He knew that God would fund any work into which He led him.

The summer work being over, Percy began to report to the churches interested in his endeavors. He spoke at the Presbyterian Church in Sooke, B.C., relating what he and the men had witnessed on the survey and the contacts they had made. He told the congregations of his intent to return to the coast the following summer, but he made no appeal for donations.

God Provides

One of the men who heard him, Horace Goodrich, managed the Sooke Harbor Fishing Company for his father. Mr. Goodrich offered Percy the use of any of the fleet of fishing boats at the dock. Percy chose the *Otter Point*, a 50-foot fish packer with a three-cylinder Union gasoline engine. Next he chose a crew: Philip Mack, the guide; Dr. Hewitt, a retired missionary doctor; Sammy Whiting, the chairman of the society; Herb Corfield, an engineer; Bill Crabb, a local businessman; Ernie Wilderspin, the secretary of the society; and Percy's son, Frank, who was then about 10 years old.

> They covered virtually every bay and inlet from Victoria to Kyoquot Sound that summer. The poverty they discovered was appalling—economically, medically, and spiritually. The doctor treated 273 people, doing dentistry as well. Used clothing was given out to the most needy, and services were held at every cannery or logging camp. Hunger for the Word of God was even greater than they had expected.[1]

While God used big gifts (such as the boat) to further Percy's work, He also used smaller gifts. In one case, a young boy heard about the need of the mission and put all of his money—two pennies—into a jar. He labeled it "For a Shantyman boat" and asked the Lord to bless the pennies. Then he hid the jar in the back of his closet. His secret was safe for only a few days, until his mother found the jar while cleaning his room. She took the jar and spread the word about the purpose of the fund. Even though money was in short supply during those Depression days, the two pennies caught the imagination of people, and they started to give. They continued giving until the jar was completely full. When the money was counted up, the fund amounted to 300 dollars. This gift started the building of the *Messenger II*.

While that fund grew, Percy spoke at other churches. It was mission policy for its members not to make an appeal for funds when they were telling of the work on the field, nor were letters of appeal to be sent out. The missionaries only reported on the work God was doing and how He was providing for the need, with the intent that He would receive all the glory. That practice still continues today. All that time, people donated enough money so that the mission's bills were paid and the missionaries received their salaries.

The appeal for funds was made to the Lord, who "owns the cattle on a thousand hills" (Ps. 50:10), by both the missionary and the prayer group that met for an hour each week to pray specifically for the missionaries, the work and the funds. The group had begun meeting about five years previously to pray for a new missionary to come and begin the work. God had provided the missionary, and so now they were praying for the funds to continue the work and pay his small stipend.

The treasurer was given the 300-dollar fund for recording. This man believed strongly in Percy's work on the west coast of the island, but it is doubtful that he had ever seen one of the trails that Percy had to hike to reach those who lived in the small, unchurched communities. He listened to Percy's rationale as to why he needed a boat to reach the many who were not near roads or trails, but he was not convinced.

In the plan of God, this man went to New Westminster one day to visit some friends. One of these friends was a young man who was an enthusiast about small boats. The young man had worked his way up to become head of a boat-building company, and as he spoke about the benefits of mission work by boat, the treasurer began to change his mind. While the two talked, the young man said his company would build a sturdy hull if the Shantymen could pay the bills for materials.

By the time the treasurer returned to Victoria, he supported the plan to build a boat. He entrusted the 300-dollar fund to Percy, who deposited it in the bank in the city of New Westminster. With faith that God would provide all the necessary funds, the work on the hull began. No one knew the extent of the final cost of this construction, but they believed that God would provide what was lacking.

Only the best of materials and tight construction would keep the ship afloat in the treacherous waters of the Pacific coast.

My Aunt Millie, who remembers those days of building the *Messenger II,* told me of watching Percy open the mail. She often heard him utter a quiet "Praise the Lord," or "Thank You, Lord," as he removed a check from a letter. It amazed her, because some of the postmarks were not local, and some even came from as far away as Australia and New Zealand. She thought of how God must have caused those people to send the check a month or two earlier so it would arrive at the time it was needed. There was no airmail then; mail from other parts of the world came the long way by ship.

Percy, along with other volunteers, began the labor of shaping steaming oak ribs and tough fir planking for the hull. The owner of the shipyard himself worked alongside the men, as he was able. Their bruised and bleeding hands were a mark of this labor of love. Slowly, the hull began to take shape.

The enthusiasm of those working on the hull was infectious to those passing by. They were curious as to what was being built, and it soon became known that a mission boat was underway. People stopped by to watch the work and check on the progress. These contacts provided another opportunity for Percy and the workers to witness about God's love, salvation and wondrous provision in this project.

Percy gave reports on the progress of the building project and gave praise to God when funds miraculously came in. As the work continued, people gave of the little they had. Just as God had fed the multitude with a boy's lunch, so in this venture the two pennies that had become 300 dollars began to increase. When a bill for the boat became due, the money was always on hand to pay it in full. When the final bill was paid, the bank account still had a balance of 400 dollars! God had truly been faithful to His promise to supply all the need.

The evening before the hull was launched, Percy drove around the neighborhood in his old Model A Ford sedan and gathered up all the youngsters who had watched them work on the boat. He let them board it and explore every inch from stern to wheelhouse. Their happy chatter rang throughout the boat, as did the clatter of their feet climbing the ladders and walking the decks. It was exciting just to watch them enjoy being on board.

The finished hull was towed across to Victoria to wait for the procurement of an engine. This was a major expense and a matter of intense prayer by all acquainted with the project. The congregation of Central Baptist Church in the city was especially interested in seeing the boat completed.

Once again, God showed His hand of provision, for one day the pastor of the church found a roll of hundred-dollar bills slipped under the door. An accompanying note stipulated that the donor remain anonymous. The amount given was enough for the new engine and the rest of the fittings required for the ship to be ready for sea. What a great time of rejoicing there was among the committee, the prayer group, the church, the missionary and the others who had given their time and labor. Their faith was strengthened as they saw the way God provided at each point of need. They realized that if He could do that for the mission society, then He could do it for them as well. Such a demonstration of God's faithfulness was necessary during that time in the middle of the Great Depression.

CHAPTER SIX

THE *MESSENGER II*
IS LAUNCHED

Those who go down to the sea in ships, Who do business in great waters, They see the works of the LORD, and His wonders in the deep.
(Ps. 107:23-24)

THE SHIP, ONCE only a dream in the eye of faith, was now a reality of wood and metal, pipes and wiring, engine and propeller. She lay quietly at her pier in the Inner Harbor of Victoria, awaiting her commissioning.

Messenger II

The words of Scripture written above were put across the finishing strip above the pilothouse windows. We did try to place before all those who saw the boat a message from the God and Father of our Lord Jesus Christ. We longed for her to be filled with the Spirit of the Lord and become a life-giving instrument in the hands of God.

(PW)

I remember that day in 1934. It was a Sunday afternoon, and I sat with family members and many others who had gathered there to dedicate this ship for God's service. There was great praise to God for His faithful backing during her construction. We sang hymns of thanksgiving. Those who spoke told of God's leading at each new step of construction, how He had brought just the right people along when they were needed, and how He had provided the funds each time when the payment was due. Then the ship was commissioned the *Messenger II* and dedicated to the work of the Lord on the Pacific coast of Vancouver Island. It was a great occasion and a real witness to every passerby who walked along the nearby causeway.

Although the bills had all been paid, God would now have to provide the money for the provisions, fuel and maintenance that would be needed to reach the inhabitants of the island. Percy and the members of the committee believed that God would continue to fund the work He had begun. The weekly prayer group added this ship and the safety of the crew to its prayer log. Whenever it sailed the stormy waters, the prayer group asked for God's protective power, endurance and safe delivery of the ship into harbor. No one will ever know how many dangers were avoided or how many storms were weathered in quiet waters as a result of those prayers.

When one considers that in the 1930s there were no electronic navigation aids to help a captain chart his course among the rocks and reefs on the coast, the months of safe voyages are a testament to God's care and direction. Percy piloted the boat in and out of inlets and bays with only the aid of marine charts, tide tables, a compass, a radio and a good pair of binoculars. The shoreline of Vancouver Island was certainly a dangerous and treacherous place. One had to know where safe harbors were all along the coastline. Storms and fog could blow in suddenly, making it necessary to find the nearest quiet water in which to anchor.

Weather forecasting, too, was in its infancy. A captain had to know how to read the signs of the wind, water and sky. Piloting a boat in the "Graveyard of the Pacific" was not for the fainthearted or recreational boater. Not even the largest freighters were immune to the 25- to 30-foot waves with spume blown by gale-force winds, much less a 32-foot boat manned by a one- or two-man crew. Every major storm left the debris of large ships and small boats along the rocks and shoals of the coast. At times, there was no indication that a ship had ever passed that way. Lives were lost at sea, and no evidence remained of those who had sailed there.

The Mission Begins

The *Messenger II* was soon ready to begin its mission. As Percy said goodbye to his family in Vancouver, Margarette kissed him and told him to go on to do what God had called him for. "I'll be all right," she said, but her heart was heavy with concern. He would be gone for weeks at a time. The prayers of his family and those of the weekly prayer group would be his support.

During his absence, the family's main contact with Percy was by letters. Mail was carried by ship up the west coast on a regular 10-day schedule. The *Princess Maquinna* made routine stops where goods, freight and mail were off-loaded and new cargo taken on. Depending on the ship's schedule, mail between Margarette and Percy could take two or three weeks. Margarette carried her worries in her heart and her prayers for Percy were ever with her, yet she never asked him to stay at home.

If Percy was in Victoria, he could talk by phone with his family in Vancouver, but long distance calls were expensive. Direct dialing was nonexistent. A telephone operator had to arrange the call. You told her the number you wanted, and she would ring it for you. If the call were long distance, she'd say she would have to call you back when the connection was completed. Then you hung up and waited for her to call. If you requested a person-to-person call, that was even more expensive.

Few people had their own phone line. It was common for families to be on a "party line," with each family having its own specific ring. You never knew who else was listening to your phone conversation. Often, listening in on the party line was a form of entertainment. It was certainly a quick way for news to get around the neighborhood.

As for Percy, the *Messenger II* was his home away from home. Its 32-foot length housed the engine room with the wheelhouse above, a few bunks, a miniscule galley and a seating area. Today, people travel in motor homes or trailers of that size fitted out with every convenience possible for their comfort. But imagine living in that small space, cooking on a small two-burner while the deck is constantly moving up and down. Imagine being alone at sea, looking out of the wheelhouse to see a storm brewing or a fog bank moving in. You have to decide quickly where to pull in out of the storm, and you pray that you can make it in time. The chart of the area could tell you compass headings and rocky obstructions at the closest place to anchor safely, but only your seamanship would actually get you into your desired haven.

We, too, have felt many a weakness as our hearts have melted in the midst of marine crises which arise so suddenly and for which often there is no solution. Always in the midst of the sudden fears, as we have appealed to God for His presence and assistance, He has come forward with His mighty power and given first peace, then power. Perhaps that is why the marine missionary falls in love with his work. He learns to love the very thing which heretofore has produced fear in his heart.

(PW)

Reaching People

When Percy began his mission on the *Messenger II*, he had already surveyed Barkley Sound the previous two summers. Now he could visit the inhabitants there and bring comfort and hope to them. This would not be just a boat ministry, but a door-to-door visitation ministry. The boat was the means to transport him to people and places he could not reach otherwise. As always, his main purpose was to tell those he met about Jesus the Savior, who loved them with an everlasting love. Percy was a fisher of men and a hunter of souls for the Lord.

If those he visited needed help, he would help them. If they needed clothing, he would provide it from the mission boxes that had been put on board for this purpose. If they wanted fellowship, he was there to visit and converse about what was going on "outside." As he sailed into new areas, he entered places where the gospel had not been preached. It was truly a pioneer work. Some were hungry for the fellowship but not ready to hear about Jesus. So he would first establish a friendship, show an interest in them as individuals, and try to be a servant of God's love. If a farmer were digging potatoes, Percy gathered them. If a man were chopping wood, he piled it up for him. If a woman was struggling with little ones, he washed the dishes or told the children stories. Whenever he saw an opportunity to give practical help, he did it without being asked. Once the people found they could trust him, opportunities came for him to talk to them about their relationship with God.

Percy also pulled into the wharves of logging camps and mining camps. This was a different kind of visit. In many instances, he was welcome as a man but not as a preacher. Yet even if he was not particularly welcome, he was seldom refused the opportunity to hold a meeting in the bunkhouse, where he would tell the men the old, old story of Jesus and His love for everyone.

A quote from a June 1976 article that Percy wrote for *Decision* magazine gives us a realistic picture of the mindset of these camps:

> Have you ever lived in a mining district where gold has been discovered in large quantities? Have you seen wide-open sin with no one to hinder or care? Have you entered a district where there is no church and no one seems to want one? We were warned to stay out of one district, but the Lord led us to enter and we did. Soon men, women and children of the logging community began to pack the hall. From the ranks of those who found Christ there, five men are now in full-time service for their blessed Lord . . .
>
> A missionary is an intruder. He is a foreign element moving into the social structure of an area, disrupting the norm. It is one thing to have evangelistic meetings in a city center with scores of churches cooperating, but it is an entirely different matter to invade an unchurched area, gather an assembly of believers, and construct a building to house them.
>
> A missionary must be prepared for a brass-knuckle type of opposition. We lost one of our young men to a drug-crazed killer, and another missionary was beaten almost to death. But sometimes the opposition is not man-made; the very elements seem to conspire against us.
>
> I have personally faced many kinds of opposition but have found that each one has added spice to my life.[1*]

Percy's trust in God had been tested and tried to the point that he could enter a situation with perfect confidence that God would

---

*This excerpt was taken from *Decision* magazine, June 1976; Billy Graham Evangelistic Association; used by permission, all rights reserved.

work it out. He often said that in the middle of a trial, he looked forward with eagerness to see how God was going to solve the problem.

> On the field amongst the working men, one is usually startled by some simple message of truth from humble workers. It was on the trail by Tsusiat Falls that we received one of our greatest lessons. We were going from the lighthouse of Pachena Point to the Indian villages at Nitinat Lake. Our companion was a trapper who was well known throughout the district.
>
> We were traveling along at a steady pace and came at last to the beautiful falls, which are a landmark to the voyagers passing that way. We stopped for our regular rest period, placing our packs upon a log from which we could take them up again when we resumed our journey.
>
> Joe was a man with an imagination, but with very little "book-larnin" to assist. As we gazed out over the glorious scene at that point, Joe said, 'You know, Pete, I think sin is mighty funny stuff. It's a lot like dynamite. I ain't exactly a-scared of it, but I got a lot of respect for it!" I do not know how that would sound to a theologian, but to me it was precious. Simple words, but a powerful message. Simple presentation, but a marvelous truth.
>
> It wasn't long afterwards that Joe found Jesus Christ as His Savior from the "dynamite," which he had learned to respect. Our last meeting was in his own home, surrounded by several of his grandchildren. When I asked him how he liked the life which he now lived by faith in the Lord Jesus, he replied, "It's just like heaven was here!"
>
> (PW)

An interesting aside to Percy's work during the mid-1930s was arranging meetings for the Reverend Michael Billester, a Russian missionary. Reverend Billester had come to Canada before World War I to seek his fortune, with the intention of returning to his village to take care of his family when he had accumulated enough money. But God had other plans for him. He was converted in Montreal and enrolled in the Ontario Bible College. After graduation, he married and became a missionary in Riga, Latvia, for two years. Later, he became the head of that same missionary organization.

Percy had an interest in politics and liked to keep abreast of what was going on in the provincial legislature. The Depression in Canada had led to some political unrest in British Columbia. The Communist party was gaining members and becoming strong enough to try for a seat in the provincial elections. It was at this time that Reverend Billester came to Victoria preaching about the dangers of Communism. As a Russian, he was well aware of the dangers of that doctrine and sought to warn Christians about it. Percy began arranging meetings for him in churches, but soon he had to move to larger venues to accommodate the crowds. Finally, the largest hall in Victoria was too small, and so they moved the meetings to Vancouver.

In one meeting, a number of Communist party members were in attendance. Reverend Billester moved to the podium, looked carefully at it, inspected the inside and outside, and finally moved it around a bit. By this time, he had the complete attention of everyone present. He looked over the audience and said in his heavy Russian accent, "I was just checking to see if there was a bomb in here." The audience chuckled, but Reverend Billester was quite serious. There had been threats on his life because of his warnings about the Communist doctrine. Percy told me later that the failure of the Communist party to get a seat in the B.C. government was attributed to the warnings that Reverend Billester had given in the 1930s.

In 1949, Reverend Michael Billester would become my father-in-law when I married his son, Robert. The mission Michael Billester took on became a major effort to reach the Slavic people in Europe and, after World War II, in South America.

Living by Faith

Whenever the *Messenger II* was due to leave for a voyage up the west coast, the necessary provisions became a matter of sincere, expectant prayer. The weekly prayer group was always kept apprised of the sailing schedule, and their prayers were joined with Percy's for God to provide everything necessary for the trip. The available funds in the treasury were not always sufficient to pay for food, gasoline, medical supplies, literature and the other unexpected expenses, but the available money, or lack of it, was never a matter of great concern to Percy. He had implicit faith that God would provide the supply by the time it was needed. And God did so, time and time again.

Percy became known as a man of great faith, but he always contended that God was a great God who loved to answer the prayers of His children. He prayed for specifics, not generalities. If a doctor were to accompany him on a trip, he would bring to God the need for certain kinds of medical instruments. If he was beginning a new building program, he would itemize in his prayers the type of lumber, the nails and screws, the concrete, the plumbing supplies and any other necessities that would be needed for the project to proceed. And as he began the project, whatever it was, the supplies would begin to arrive and kept pace with the need.

> At one time the needs had exceeded the income by several hundreds of dollars, and the leaders were becoming concerned. As usual, the [prayer] luncheon group was advised and asked to pray particularly for God to send His merciful aid. The field force was also called to prayer and all the friends were invited to join with them.
>
> As near as we could discern, two days later a letter was received at our head office in Toronto, advising them that a gift of four thousand dollars in government bonds was at hand, specified for the west coast work, where the need was great. The gift had

come from a woman of whom we had never heard. She had heard of the particular district where the need was, but she did not know of the need nor how to reach the missionaries there.

Later, it evolved that the donor was an elderly woman nearing the end of her days, who had fallen heir to a fortune which had been left by her brother. One day she had been praying and asking the Lord to reveal what she should do with the money, when God spoke plainly to her and told her to send the above amount to the Shantymen. This she immediately did, knowing nothing of the needs of the mission, as she lived in a small village three thousand miles away.

(PW)

One time when Percy was at sea, he and the others on board had only eaten fish for many days, and they hungered for a good, succulent beef roast. At their next port, one of the cooks at the camp said he couldn't give them anything, but he asked if they would like a piece of beef. He went to the refrigerator, cut off a huge roast and gave it to them. Soon the wonderful aroma of roasting meat was coming from the galley. That night they feasted on the beef, savoring every juicy mouthful. They gave grateful thanks to God "who gives us richly all things to enjoy" (1 Tim. 6:17).

Some people on the coast have few visitors, and when they do, it is a time for a cup of tea, or a meal, and conversation. On one occasion, over a cup of tea, my companions and I were informed that we were the first missionaries to enter their community since they themselves had arrived some seventeen years before. The day before, the little group had prayed that God would send them a missionary, as they were so hungry for a spiritual contact.

Finally, one of the men said that he would have given much indeed to have had a missionary at hand when his father had died. The son had to make a rough wooden box, dig the grave, and bury the remains of his father. Then he read from the Bible and the prayer book as he paid his last respects.

He told us, "I would have given much to have had a mission-ary on hand at that time. And what is more, when I read of all the thousands of dollars that are being raised for missionary work on the quiet waters inside the island, I was just bitter to think of how we are neglected on this 'Graveyard of the Pacific.'"

On another day, the *Messenger II* pulled into a small bay where a number of fishermen lived who hole-up for the winter and spend long hours during the other seasons trolling on the Pacific. As my companion and I approached one shack, the host invited us in.

After a time of chatting on serious things, and some not so serious, and after a cup of tea, it was time for the two to depart. The kindly host speeded the departure with, "I'm so glad you came to visit me. I've only had two visitors in the last year. It's great to have strangers drop in, even if they are missionaries!"

(PW)

CHAPTER SEVEN

THE STRANGER'S REST

*I was hungry and you gave Me food; I was thirsty and you gave Me
drink; I was a stranger and you took Me in . . . and the King will
answer and say to them, "Assuredly, I say to you, inasmuch as you
did it to one of the least of these My brethren, you did it to Me."*
(Matthew 25:35,40)

THE GREAT DEPRESSION was deepening in Canada. There
were almost no jobs to be had, except the rare opening in a
large company. Men had begun to leave the smaller towns
in hopes of getting employment in the nearest big city. When that
effort failed, they continued their search by "riding the rails" to the
next city. By hitchhiking or traveling in the railway boxcars, the men
extended their search westward or eastward. When they reached
Vancouver and still found no work, they made their way across
the Georgia Straits to Vancouver Island, where several logging and
mining camps were located.

The logging and mining industries were major employers in the
province of British Columbia, but they were beginning to shut down
as well. A few men found work, and they considered themselves

lucky. Most did not, however, and they continued their search on the island. When the seekers reached Port Alberni, a mill town, they came to the end of their journey. If they did not find work there, there were no other options available to them.

By this time, Percy was much better acquainted with the area of his mission, for the *Messenger II* gave him greater reach to those on the coastline. In Port Alberni he saw the misery and hopelessness of the unemployed. There was no source of income for them, no welfare and no unemployment insurance. The men were destitute, so they could not send money home to their families, who were waiting hopefully for assistance. No public agency was prepared or willing to tackle the problem of assisting the hordes of men who landed in their city.

Percy saw a new opportunity for God to meet the needs of these drifters. His own heart yearned to tackle the problems faced by the homeless men, and he made the answer a matter of earnest and specific prayer. He approached the town fathers and asked them what they planned to do about the homeless men. One of the leaders turned to him and said, "Why don't you do something?" Percy countered, "Give me a lot, and I will." So they agreed to his request and gave him a lot. It was full of debris, logs, stumps, garbage and rusty metal.

The next morning, Percy went and stood on the lot. He envisioned a building where the men in distress could be sheltered and fed. As he stood there, he prayed that God would be honored in the building, and he claimed by faith the souls of the men who would be housed in it. He prayed that broken hearts and lives would be mended by the touch of Almighty God and that when they left, they would go regenerated by the love of God.

As he stood there alone in the rain, he prayed, "Oh, God, because this work is to bring glory to Yourself, confirm it this morning by sending someone here with money so we can start to build."[1] Just then a car drove up, and the driver called out to him.

Percy recognized the driver's voice and joined him in the car. The friend told him he had a check waiting for him in his office. When they arrived, the man gave Percy a check made out for 50 dollars. That was a large sum in those days, and Percy took it as a token of God's further provision for the building. Once more, God had shown Himself faithful to His Word.

Percy's friend was the manager of the local mill. When Percy told him of his vision, his friend said to go down to the lumber stacks and the foreman would fix him up. The two men went through the piles, selecting the lumber. The foreman said, "You can have this lumber for five dollars a thousand board feet if you get a truck here right away." The lumber was soon loaded on a borrowed truck and deposited on the lot. The building got underway once the lot was cleared, and within a short time the dormitory-like structure was ready for occupancy. It was called "The Stranger's Rest."

The public was pleased, and the civic officials attended the opening with a right good will. But the work to be carried on was basically a gospel work, and many resented the fact.

Suddenly letters began to appear in the paper. The most virulent were anonymous and attacked with great fury. These letters were aimed at the missionary [myself], and the aim was good. Soon the press began to print articles which only added fuel to the flames.

Wisely, the missionary did not retaliate, but went quietly on his way, ministering to the needs of the destitute, even though his heart was sore from injustice and falsehood. One day the phone rang, and the editor of the local paper asked the missionary to visit his office. When the two men were closeted privately, the editor said, "I have been publishing letters and articles against you, but I have been watching your reaction, and I find that we have been wrong. I want to apologize, and say that no further articles will appear, except those that will aid your work."

(PW)

In the first 18 months of The Stranger's Rest operation, more than 11,000 men came through its doors. At times when Percy was in town, he would visit the building and find as many as 36 men at a time sleeping wherever they could—in chairs, on the floor, or under the tables—just so they were out of the cold and wet weather. Percy told me that in all the time the doors were open for the men, only two blankets were stolen.

Every man who came into The Stranger's Rest was presented with the gospel message and told of his need for salvation. Many did accept the Lord as Savior, so the building became a gospel center as well as a welfare center. Another of Percy's visions to be of service to mankind had come into being.

Once this place was in operation, a local committee was formed to oversee the work. The Shantymen did not support a stationary project such as The Stranger's Rest. As one of their missionaries, Percy was to be an itinerant, visiting from door to door or village to village, always telling those he met of the wonderful love of Jesus.

CHAPTER EIGHT

THE HOSPITAL

*"I will feed My flock, and I will make them lie down," says the
Lord God. "I will seek what was lost and bring back what was
driven away, bind up the broken and strengthen what was sick."*
(Ezekiel 34:15-16)

ANOTHER OF PERCY'S concerns during the early years on
the *Messenger II* was the great lack of medical help for the
people of Vancouver Island. For more than 200 miles along
the coastline, there was no first-aid station, no medical clinic, no
resident doctor and no hospital.

Before the *Messenger II* had been built, Percy had taken a trip
aboard the *Otter Point* and covered the whole area from Victoria
to Kyoquot Sound. He and the crew had been appalled at the
economic, medical and spiritual poverty they encountered, and the
severe lack of even basic needs had ignited a deep desire in Percy to
do something about the situation. He first began to pray earnestly
about the need, asking for God's wisdom and direction on how to
proceed. On future voyages, he sometimes had a doctor on board
who attended to people wherever they pulled into port.

He began to pray earnestly for a doctor who would move to the west coast of Vancouver Island and establish a medical work. At one point he heard of a doctor who prayed for his patients, and even had the temerity to pray, "Oh, God, if you can't send me to Africa—then let me go to the toughest place on the west coast!" Percy thought this was just the man for the job. He knew where the "toughest place on the west coast" was. He sent a wire to the doctor, who was in Vancouver, and invited him to attend the Shantymen's annual day of prayer in Victoria.

Neither of the men had met previously. The doctor wondered how he would identify the missionary, but as soon as the two men spied each other, there was no hesitation in their greeting. Percy brought the young doctor, Herman Alexander McLean, M.D. (known as "Doc") to the meeting and introduced him to the group. The doctor sensed the sweet presence of God as the prayers were offered. After the meeting, Percy invited Doc to go with him on his next trip up the coast. He said, "I have made plans to leave in *Messenger II* at 1:00 P.M. on Monday—one week from tomorrow!"

Doc said he would have to check with the hospital and arrange for leave. Percy assured him that God could easily arrange that. When Doc went back to Vancouver and asked for the time off, the hospital superintendent allowed him to take it. Doc met Percy on the appointed day.

Going to God for Necessities

As they boarded the boat, Doc saw no provisions. He wondered if there was even gas in the tanks. In the morning, Percy asked if he could borrow five cents to buy milk for breakfast, which caused the doctor to question if this undertaking was such a good idea. Next, Percy asked him if he had brought his medical instruments, to which Doc replied that they were still in storage in Alberta, where he had spent a year in Bible study. During his time in Vancouver, he had used the hospital equipment.

"Well, then," said Percy, "let's pray about it." The two men knelt in prayer, asking God to provide these necessities. As they rose, Percy looked out a porthole and saw a Red Cross sign on a building. He told the doctor to go up there and see if they would give him some bandages and dressings to take along.

The Red Cross superintendent met Doc and told him to select whatever supplies he needed from the displays in the store. Doc began to choose bandages and supplies and also essential instruments such as a blood pressure machine, an oralscope and others. He next selected boxes of medicines and drugs, all the while wondering how he was going pay for it. The total amount came to more than 150 dollars! When he asked the superintendent that question, the man replied, "Just charge it to the Red Cross!"

The doctor was elated! "Charge it to the Red Cross" sang in his mind as he thought of the cross of Calvary, where God shed His blood for man's salvation. He hurried back to the boat and excitedly related to Percy all the details of this wonderful encounter. In a new way, he had experienced God's miraculous provision for His work, even when there was no money to pay the bill.

Percy listened patiently, and when Doc was finished he said, "Just look around and see what else God has done while you were away." Doc looked and saw full cupboards, stored packages and filled gas tanks. There was even extra money on hand for expenses along the way.

Precisely at one o'clock, the ship slipped her moorings and pulled away from the wharf. They were on their way to "the toughest place on the west coast." At every stop, people came for medical aid. They begged the doctor to stay in their town and open a clinic there. But the *Messenger II* pushed on to the next stop, where the same scene was repeated.

The farther up the coast they went, the greater the medical need they encountered. There was no aid of any kind and no telephones for the people to signal when they needed help. The depth of the need was greater than Doc had ever imagined.

After two months of seeing such staggering needs, Doc said to Percy, "This is the place God wants me!" Percy assured him that he would support him morally and spiritually in any way he could, but that Doc would have to arrange the financial support for himself and his family.

The Right Place

Percy moored in an area of Nootka Island and set out in a small rowboat to investigate the coastline. He soon found what he was looking for. Just west of Ceepeecee in Hecate Channel, a fairly level piece of land jutted from the mountainside out into the sea. It had a southern exposure, so that every bit of sunshine would brighten it during the long winter days. Most important, a good stream of pure water flowed down to the spot.[1]

Even though they did not have title to the land or even one penny to build on it, both men felt the urgency of the need. The building would need to be put up during the summer, for construction would have to stop when the rains came. As for the land title, they would put the building on skids so that it could be moved off if their application were turned down.

The two men knelt in prayer one morning, asking God for guidance in planning for the next step and for the funds to begin. God led them to cross the bay to a small mill to see what it would cost to erect a small building about 14 by 32 feet. When they started looking over the stacks of lumber, the foreman approached them to see what they wanted. He was an angry man and suffering a bad hangover from the previous night's binge. When he learned the purpose for the lumber, he let loose a string of profanities, saying he was not interested in building a mission hospital.

Percy and Doc had heard this type of rejection before and did not turn to leave. Percy said, "I didn't ask you if you were interested in mission hospitals; I asked you for the price of the lumber." Finally, the foreman told them to come back in half an hour. When they returned, the manager himself met them.

"What do you want the lumber for?" he said. When the two told him, he asked, "How soon do you want to start?"

"Right away," they replied.

Hoping to get rid of them quickly, the manager said, "I'll give you the lumber if you'll get it out of here this morning."[2]

With the realization that God had provided the lumber for free, and using the energy born of victory, Percy and Doc dumped the lumber in the bay and lashed it into bundles. The *Messenger II* then towed the bundles across to the hospital site. Despite not owning the title or having even one red cent, work on the hospital began.

Volunteer labor came in from men who were out of work at the nearby fishing camp. In appreciation for their help, Doc agreed to pay for their meals at the bunkhouse when summer was over. By August, the land had been cleared and the building was almost completed. Doc turned his energies to getting equipment and furnishings. Another more pressing need was for nurses to assist in the hospital operation.

Just before Percy left on the *Messenger II,* Doc talked to him about this need. Doc wanted to write to some nurses who might be interested in serving in this mission endeavor. But Percy said, "No, Doc. God knows the nurses He wants up here. He'll send them."

That fall, a fully trained nurse applied to work in the new hospital. A friend of hers, who was also a nurse, felt God calling her to the coast, so the two of them arrived together. A young man had also heard of this outpost hospital and wanted to join it. The three of them boarded the same boat for the same journey. Also among the passengers was Doc's family, who had stayed in the Victoria area while the hospital was being built.

During this time, Doc McLean's family had been living in Sidney, just north of Victoria. One day the baby, Garth, swallowed a prune pit and was in extreme pain. Percy was in Victoria at the time, and when he heard about the baby, he hurriedly drove to the McLean home. The family gathered with him, and the matter was brought to the Lord in prayer for His healing. A few days later, Garth had returned to his normal self, and a grateful family praised God for His intervention.[3]

A Surprising New Home

On November 4, 1937, Mrs. McLean and their children arrived aboard a fish packer. As the vessel turned from Tahsis Narrows into the opening of Hecate Channel, the skipper said, "We'll soon be there now." The McLean children at that time—Max, Donnel, Shirley, Bruce and baby Garth—excitedly scanned the shorelines on both sides of the channel, competing to be the first to see the new hospital with their dad waving at them from the shore. Finally, the motor slowed. "This is Esperanza," the skipper announced. For a moment the family was hushed. All they could see were two small shacks. Their most imaginative dreams could not have foreseen such a dismal scene. Surrounding the shacks was dense underbrush; towering above the underbrush were enormous fir and hemlock trees; and close behind were steep, rock-faced mountains.[4]

One can only imagine their shock as they viewed the place that was to be their home for the next several years. A great deal of manual labor would be required from everyone. Every bit of wood for heating had to be chopped, and every drop of water had to be brought from the nearby creek. At first, there was no electricity for lighting—just oil lamps— and the cool weather provided the only refrigeration.

Supplies came in every 10 days when the *Princess Maquinna* brought what had been ordered. The McLeans had to bake their own bread, and canned goods provided their milk, vegetables, fruits and some meat products. (As a young girl, I felt sorry for the McLean children because they had to drink canned milk. I had no idea of the real hardships they all worked through!)

Mrs. McLean felt the loneliness keenly, and prayer became her lifeline for strength to face the daily tasks. She realized that when her husband had asked to be sent to the toughest place on the west coast, God had answered that prayer. Yet she resolved to be a partner with him in that place of difficulty.

The next year, a second story was added to the hospital, providing eight more beds and an operating room. Even that addition was stretched to the limit by the increase in the number of patients requiring hospitalization. In 1939, the hospital was overcrowded, and more beds were required. The family and hospital staff prayed for God's leading on whether to build a new, larger hospital, and God answered by a letter from the Shantymen's headquarters in Toronto. It contained a promise of 4,000 dollars that had been designated for the hospital.

In accordance with this funding, construction started and the new hospital opened in August of 1939. During the opening ceremonies, the doctor announced that the building was completely debt free. In its first six months of operation, more than 150 patients had been treated.[5]

While I was in Esperanza recently to attend a business meeting, I talked with Donnel McLean and his sisters, Shirley Sutherland, Dorothy McLean and Lois Hooks. Shirley mentioned the time the *Messenger II* visited and Percy gave her a doll in a bassinette. That gift was a treasure to her as a young child. Her sister Lois mentioned to me that when she saw Margarette knitting on a Sunday afternoon, she realized that such a benign occupation was allowed on the Lord's Day. In those days, godly people were careful not to work on Sunday. They spent the time between church services quietly reading their Bible, visiting friends or walking.

Tragedy Hits

The hospital continued to expand, with more buildings erected to house the staff and the doctor's family, which now included eight children (Dorothy, Ruth and Lois were born at Esperanza). Dr. McLean would occasionally quip that he had "two and a half-dozen children." Many lives were saved, both physically and spiritually, during the years the hospital was in operation. Some were comforted in a ward while their life ebbed to a close. Prayer for God's wisdom and guiding hand in each procedure was always spoken over each patient.

In October 1948, Dr. McLean and his son Bruce went to Chamiss Bay to retrieve the *Messenger II*, which had been donated to the hospital when the *Messenger III* began service with the Shantymen's Mission. The boat had been left at Chamiss Bay because of a bad winter storm that prevented them from sailing it back to Esperanza.

The two men flew to Chamiss Bay and boarded the boat. They left there just after noon for the trip home, but soon found themselves in rough waters. A new storm had arisen with howling winds, and the pilothouse was battered by every wave that came in. Bruce became very ill, while Doc tried vainly to keep the boat upright in the seas. This desperate situation lasted for several hours until just about dark. They were only about 15 minutes from home when the motor quit. Doc found that the gas line and the bilge had filled up with water. He attempted to clear the line and pump the bilge several times, but to no avail. They were in danger of being blown onto the rocks. Doc knew that there was nothing left to do but abandon ship.

Doc and Bruce clambered out on the deck, trying to move to the side away from the rocks, when a huge breaker took the ship into the air. The two men fell into the water between the boat and the rocks. There was no chance to say goodbye or stay together. Doc came to the surface just at the point of drowning. He saw Bruce, but knew that his son was dead.

Doc's own situation was extremely perilous. Now he was at the mercy of the waves and again in danger of drowning. Just then, another wave washed over him and left him on a rock. He clung to it with desperate, clawing fingers. Another wave came. As it receded, he climbed higher and clung on tightly as yet another waved crashed over him. With each receding wave, he managed to climb to the pinnacle of the rock where he held on for dear life, being battered by the waves about every five minutes.

Finally, when daybreak came, he saw that in the mercy of God, the *Messenger II* had been lifted over the rocks and was impaled on the side away from the storm. When the tide was lower, he left his refuge in the rock cleft and went over to the boat to retrieve food and blankets. He did not know if he would be rescued or would die there on the rocks. He entrusted himself to God.

Doc spent another night with another high tide and more waves, but this time he tied himself to the rock with ropes retrieved from the boat. He was able to eat some food he had taken from the boat. On the third day, through straining eyes, he thought he saw smoke on the horizon. It was his rescuer, a vessel of the Kyuquot Trollers Association. He began to frantically wave a sheet in the air so he could be seen. The ship turned toward him, and he was saved at last!

While he felt deep grief that Bruce had died, he also felt reborn and glad that God still had a purpose for him. All these strong emotions burst forth in weeping as he set foot on the deck of the ship. To quote Dr. McLean as he returned home, "The tragic loss of our son left us with deep scars. Perhaps he was the sacrifice we had to endure in order to carry out God's work."[6]

As Doc was struggling to stay alive on the rock, Percy and Harold Peters were in the *Messenger III*. They had faced the same storm but had been able to find a sheltered cove where they could anchor in safety until the storm passed. Margarette and I were in a gospel meeting in Victoria when an usher came in and told us the news of Dr. McLean and Bruce. We hurriedly left for home, wondering whether Percy was safe. No one had heard from him, and we did not know his whereabouts. We learned the next day that he was safe and that all was well with the boat.

The December 1948 issue of the *Nootka Mission Review* reported the following words of thanks from the McLean family:

> Mr. Percy Wills and Harold Peters aboard the *Messenger III* heard the S.O.S. of the Nootka Mission Hospital Association, after the tragedy of October 2nd. With all haste they headed to the mission and brought to them such help and comfort, as only they knew how. They spent many days with them at that time and filled many needful places. May God abundantly bless them, as we feebly offer our thanks.
>
> Mrs. McLean, the doctor, and their family wish also to express their thanks to the hundreds of praying and interested friends who showed their concern by wire, flowers, letters, and gifts. Truly, words are inadequate to state the amount of encouragement, consolation, and assurance that was brought to them. It is with genuine heartfelt thanks we have these words printed. Their prayer is "God make us worthy and ever aid us to be faithful in the task that Thou hast called us to."

The hospital continued to serve the surrounding area and to attract new medical personnel. One of these was a new physician, Dr. Madeline Gereluk, who arrived in 1962. She recently wrote me to tell of meeting her husband, Joe McPherson, when he was hired as a steam engineer to maintain the boats, water system and power plant.

They were married a year later at the hospital, with Percy and Reverend Holmes from Victoria officiating at the ceremony. It was a lovely warm summer day, and a large group of friends from the hospital, the logging camps and the villages attended. When Percy had pronounced them man and wife, he leaned over to Joe and said, "Okay, Joe, this is it. Kiss her before I do." That brought a good laugh from the audience.

Nettle Soup

Madeline also told of a visit from Percy and Harold Peters one day just as supper was being served at the hospital. She and Joe were getting ready to join the group when Percy knocked on the door. The two men entered their home, and Harold was holding a bunch of stinging nettles he had just picked from around the nearby bushes.

Madeline asked if they would be eating at the hospital, but Percy said, "No, we are eating at your house with you." She was taken aback but began opening some cans of vegetables and peeling potatoes. Percy and Harold got busy cutting up the nettles and made a big pot of "nettle soup." They put salt and pepper, flour and onions in the soup, and when it was served, it was pronounced delicious.

(This "nettle soup" intrigued me when I read the letter, especially when I found stinging nettles growing in my flowerbed. I decided to see if I could find a recipe on the Internet. I did and was relieved to find that the stinging would be neutralized in the cooking. I picked the nettles and washed them, followed the recipe, and wound up with a small pot of soup. It was a deep green color and quite tasty. I think I'll make it again when the weeds grow back in the flowerbed.)

The hospital continued in operation until early 1972, when the board of directors decided to close it. There was now medical service available in Tahsis, and the provincial government felt that funding for hospital expansion would be better spent there. A committee was formed to determine a successor to Dr. McLean when he announced his retirement. The unanimous choice to lead the mission for the next phase of its ministry was Earl Johnson, a man who had worked with Percy and Harold Peters on the *Messenger III*. He knew the coastal people and was an able administrator.

At the annual spring conference that year, Dr. McLean passed the responsibility of the mission to Earl, who accepted the position of superintendent of Nootka Mission.[7]

CHAPTER NINE

THE WAR YEARS

And you will hear of wars and rumors of wars.
See that you are not troubled . . .
(Matthew 24:6)

O N SEPTEMBER 3, 1939, Percy, Margarette, Frank and I were enjoying a Sunday afternoon visit with our friends in Auburn, Washington, when the radio announcer broke into the programming with the news that Britain had declared war on Germany and its allies, Italy and Japan. We hurriedly said our goodbyes and headed for Vancouver. At that time, Canada was part of the British empire and was included in the declaration of war.

Germany moved quickly, swallowing up country after country in its blitzkrieg of Europe. Its occupation was swift and complete. Britain found itself threatened with takeover. Canada geared up rapidly for the war effort. Men were drafted, and volunteers added to their number.

The day after we got home, Percy volunteered for the army. The recruiter told him he was too old and should find some other way to aid the war effort. He found his avenue of service with the Soldiers' and Airmen's Christian Association (SACA). This organization had been formed to provide a place near a military base where the service men and women could spend their leave time without having to frequent the many bars that sprang up in the towns.

Percy's home city of Victoria was a strategic location for the war effort, with Canadian and British encampments for all three services. The large dry dock at the navy base became particularly important after Singapore fell to the Japanese early in the war. All in all, Victoria's population swelled greatly after the service bases were manned.

A New Assignment

In early 1940, Percy took a leave from the Shantymen's mission in order to work with SACA. He looked for appropriate housing for his family and the servicemen who would come. He found what he was looking for at 2024 Belmont Avenue. It was a large house on two lots, only two blocks from the streetcar line and just right for the work in which his family would be involved. The rent was 50 dollars per month. Percy received a monthly stipend from the organization, but the rest of the money needed for everyday expenses came from donations as God directed churches and individuals to give.

Percy named the home "Emmaus," which means "God with us." The family certainly needed God with them for that venture. They dedicated the house to God and asked Him to bless every person who came through the door. They prayed that those who were Christians would be encouraged and that those who were not believers would be won to the Lord by the witness they saw. God did bless their efforts, and many were encouraged and saved.

The home had large rooms, capable of seating many people for meetings or get-togethers. Upstairs were four large bedrooms, two for Percy's family and two for overnight guests. Each of the

2024 Belmont Avenue

guest rooms had four single cots, which were frequently filled. There was only one bathroom, but at least the toilet was separate from the tub and basin. Only once do I remember a lineup for the toilet. Someone had exited and left the light on and the door closed. Finally, one enterprising young man decided to try the door. So much for the lineup!

The kitchen had a nice feature: a hand basin in a niche near the stove. The pantry separated the kitchen and dining room. The huge living room was 30 feet long with a large fireplace. Two window seats along the wall frequently did double duty as beds when all the cots were taken.

The full basement had a game room of the same dimensions as the living room above it. A pool table stood in the middle, with a couple of sets of cues hanging on the wall. This was a wonderful addition to the home, and many a night the men enjoyed a game or two while others watched and cheered them on.

This was an ideal setup for the new work, except for one thing: all the walls on the main floor had dark wood paneling that extended about four feet up from the floor, even in the kitchen. Margarette looked at that and said she would not move in until the kitchen was painted. Percy promptly painted it a light green, which brightened it considerably.

Although the house was large, it had a welcoming air provided by the Spirit of God, who was the first to be welcomed. In contrast to the crowded barracks and mess halls, the warmth of family life pervaded its rooms. The large yard with many fruit trees, flowering bushes and even a chicken coop reminded the visiting servicemen of home. The rigid schedule of military life gave way to the normal times of family life while they were there.

Margarette and Percy decided not to move to Victoria until the end of my school year in June. My brother, Frank, left school and got a job until he was old enough to enlist in the Air Force. When school was out, we moved to our new home. The bedroom

I occupied had an adjacent sun porch, where I loved to sleep in good weather. I could open the double windows and see the stars. In the winter I often went to sleep lulled by the rain and the sound of foghorns.

Once we were settled and the home opened, it did not take long for the servicemen to find our place. There was no other place for the Christians in the service to gather during their hours off base.

A Home Away from Home

To the servicemen, Margarette and Percy were "Mom" and "Pop," and I was their "kid sister." It meant so much to these men and women, who were taken so quickly from their homes and neighborhoods, to spend time with a caring family. No one was ever turned away. No charge was made for meals or overnight stay. There was a general air of warmth, fellowship and good humor without criticism.

The move to Victoria provided a new kind of experience for the three of us. For the first time in my life, I had my father home every single day, rather than a few days separated by weeks on the mission boat. I was able to get to know my dad, and not just as someone to be good for.

Those years in "Emmaus" were a young girl's dream situation. I was just into my teens, and there were so many young men coming to the house every day. While I was like a kid sister to them, I developed a case of puppy love for a few of them. One night, a soldier invited me to go roller skating with him. Percy said we could go, and then added, "I'll stay there and watch you skate until you fall down." I made sure I stayed on my feet! It did not occur to me that I was being chaperoned.

We soon settled into a daily routine, much like any other family, except that we had guests every evening, with some staying overnight and into the next day. We never knew how many would come to the door and step into our loving home atmosphere.

Margarette and Percy Wills

Saturday was baking day. Margarette's cookies filled the house with wonderful aromas. She made several kinds, depending on the ingredients available. Because sugar, butter and shortening were rationed, she was adept at substitutions. Like many other housewives at that time, she used filtered chicken or beef fat in her baking. Of course, it was hard to disguise its flavor in the cookies, but after all they were home baked. That was a real plus for those who usually ate in a mess hall.

On one occasion, Margarette found that some homemade strawberry jam had started to ferment, so she used the jam in place of some of the sugar in the cookie recipe. That weekend, one of the English men asked her what she had used to sweeten the cookies. "I used some strawberry jam instead of sugar," she replied. "Oh, Mrs. Wills," he said, "In England we sometimes have sugar, but never jam!" Margarette later confessed that she didn't want to tell him it was going bad.

Percy stayed close to the Lord, a practice he maintained throughout his life. He made his decisions about what to do, where to go and who to see through quiet prayer and thought. He made sure the house rules were followed and kept a benevolent eye on all that went on. Practical jokes were sometimes perpetrated, but Percy did not discourage them. He just made sure they didn't get out of hand or go too far. He would not allow the men to use the current slang terms for women, such as "she's a real tomato" or "what a doll!"

Some of the young men wanted to discuss spiritual issues with Percy. Questions arose, and they sought godly counsel from a godly man. Margarette was also a calming and steady influence on many of these young people who had suddenly been uprooted from their homes and churches. She took a motherly interest in the men and women who were far from their families, and they responded to her caring heart.

Margarette and Percy were a team who loved the Lord and each other deeply and who worked well together. Often he gave Margarette a hug and kiss, saying, "I love you, Mama."

Both were good cooks. They could make a tasty meal out of a few leftovers. It was quite a challenge to prepare a meal for, say, six people and stretch it to feed nine, ten or more, as frequently happened. Percy was as adept at housework as was Margarette. It was not unusual to see him in an apron with a tea towel slung over his shoulder. Percy

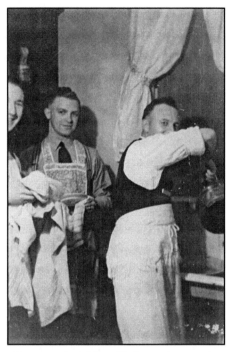

Percy and unidentified servicemen in the pantry

kept the furnace going in winter and did the yard work, while Margarette did the ironing and baking. Whatever duties needed to be done were tackled with the hearts of a servant to the family and guests.

At times, an eager young Christian would question Percy about the eternal security of the believer. Percy would not be drawn into a discussion pro or con. He simply replied that the Scripture says, "He that hath the Son, hath life" (1 John 5:12, KJV) and pointed out that the verb used was in the present tense. That statement closed the door to any possible argument. He did not allow Scripture on divisive issues to be discussed or argued. His purpose in life was to lift up Jesus Christ and salvation through His blood shed at Calvary. He did both by his manner of life as well as by speaking a word when he saw the need for it.

Just as on the mission field, whenever Percy saw a need at "2024," he would try to meet it. He knew the servicemen needed to be integrated into a fellowship with other young people, and to this end he asked the churches to announce a "Sing-Song" at our home following the Sunday evening service. Initially, each church group sat separately, but they soon got to know each other and mingled freely. They sang choruses and read letters from friends who had been transferred to other posts. Some gave a testimony of God's grace or told a new spiritual truth they had discovered in the Word of God. Those evening times closed a day dedicated to the Lord.

Refreshments were a must before the evening ended. Percy brewed coffee in a large preserving kettle. He poured a pound of coffee (no decaf was available then) into the water and boiled it, and then added an eggshell to settle the grounds. His sister Bessie donated a large loaf cake each week, and Margarette's cookies were served. The coffee was good, and few cookies or pieces of cake were left on the serving plates.

The young men soon realized another benefit to these Sunday night gatherings: attractive Christian girls who needed to be escorted home. The families with cars had to conserve gas, which was rationed. Streetcars ran frequently and were only a short walk from the house. Soon it was evident that one young man was routinely escorting a certain young lady. These Sunday night Sing-Songs continued until the home closed at the end of the war.

News from the Front

The war news was not good. Percy constantly listened to the radio as he went about his duties in the house, praying silently. He remembered the battles in the trenches in World War I. He remembered what it was like to be on the front lines. He realized Britain's desperate situation and the consequences of German occupation if the Axis coalition won.

Britain was frequently bombed by the Nazi warplanes. When the air raid sirens sounded, people left home and ran to their local shelter. There, they would huddle together until the "all clear" sound was heard. Many left the shelter to return to a home that was only rubble.

British Commonwealth forces fought bravely but barely held their own. America did not enter the war until December 1941, although some volunteers were already fighting overseas. Many times, the Axis forces seemed to be invincible, and every church offered up fervent prayers for our troops. From time to time, a day of prayer would be announced when people gathered to petition God for His mercy and ask Him to change the course of the battles.

Early in the war, the tragic battle at Dunkirk called for a retreat. The British forces were caught between the German army and the English Channel. The "bulldog" spirit of the English people showed up when every owner who could power up a boat crossed the English Channel to pick up as many troops as his boat could hold and take them back to safety in England.

Percy would not allow the sadness and gloom of the war to permeate the quiet, restful atmosphere in their home. He prayed that God would show him what could be done to lift their spirits. His answer was to announce a monthly party, or "fun night." On those occasions, the house would be filled with people, some even sitting on the stairs, watching over the banister. They participated in games or skits and, of course, singing. Refreshments were a must as well.

One memorable fun night, Percy decided to do a skit called "The Operation." A sheet was hung across the darkened room, and a strong light behind it cast a shadow on the sheet. Everyone stood around watching the simulated "operation" taking place behind the sheet. The part removed in the "operation" would be handed around the curtain into the hand of the first person, who would then pass it to the next person until all the "parts" were removed and the operation was completed. At that point, the lights came on and we could see what we held in our hands.

The usual substitutions were pieces of fruit or cooked vegetables simulating the organs that had been cut out. But Percy had another idea. (Did you know he had a well-developed sense of humor?) He knew a butcher in town and was able to get the real animal parts from him. In the darkness, when the "part" was passed around, it was assumed to be something innocuous. However, when the lights came on this night, the people were quite shocked when they saw what was in their hands. One young woman looked and promptly fainted. That was the last time that particular game was played!

Illness Strikes

A sudden serious and heart-wrenching event occurred one summer night. Awakened by unusual activity in my folks' bedroom, I went to see what happened. Margarette had had a heart attack, and Percy was ministering to her. He seemed calm in spite of the crisis. One moment she was panting for air, and he opened the window; the next, she was too cold, and he closed it. This happened several times, and I became frightened. My father quietly told me to go back to bed. I didn't really know what was going on, but Daddy's calm manner allowed me to go back to sleep.

Years later, Percy told me what had happened that night. Suspecting the seriousness of Margarette's condition, Percy had suggested that they thank and praise God for all He had done for them in the past. Neither knew what lay immediately ahead, but they clung together in their mutual love. As they waited for the doctor to arrive, they recalled the many instances when God had met their needs. Even in this tenuous time of uncertainty, their faith and trust in God's immediate care was strong. Then Percy committed her into God's care, and they left the answer in His hands.

The doctors were very concerned about Margarette's prognosis, knowing that her overactive thyroid had taxed and weakened her heart. They decided to send her to a specialist in Vancouver who was experienced in thyroid surgery. The doctor admitted her to the hospital for 10 days of complete bed rest before the operation. She was not allowed to get up, read a newspaper or do anything else that would cause excitement to her heart during that period.

In the meantime, word got around to the churches about Margarette's condition, and people all over the city began to pray for her recovery and comfort for the family. Her sister Millie came to stay with us while they were gone, and other friends took on some of the other household duties. This allowed the home to stay open and maintain its ministry to the service personnel.

Margarette's body temperature was cooled in order to minimize the effect of the general anesthesia and the stress on her heart during surgery. The operation was a success, and she spent several days recovering in the hospital. She was then taken to Grandmother's house to recuperate. I also went to stay with my grandmother while my mother was recuperating.

Because she now had no thyroid gland, and because her body temperature had been lowered for the surgery, Margarette felt the cold keenly, even though it was summer. I clearly remember coming into the house to cool off after I had been playing outside. There was Mother, lying on the sofa in her flannel pajamas, a hot water bottle at her feet under an eiderdown quilt. Just looking at her made me feel hot, but she felt barely warm.

We stayed with Grandmother while the doctor adjusted Mother's thyroid medication to the proper dosage. When she was stable, we returned to Victoria, and Margarette slowly resumed her tasks under Percy's watchful care.

Once they were back home and Margarette was feeling better, Percy was even more solicitous of her health. He made sure she got enough rest and did not overtax herself. She slowly recovered, and the routine of the home again took hold. All the servicemen were so happy to have "Mom" back again.

A Refreshing Break

In early 1943, even with Percy's continuing care for her, Margarette was wearing down under the pressure of coping with all the activities, meals and comings and goings of so many people in their home every night. Percy felt she needed a vacation, but he didn't know where she could go for a few days.

At that time, Reverend Michael Billester was holding meetings in Victoria. Percy knew him from having worked with him during the 1930s, and when Reverend Billester heard about Margarette's need, he offered to take her and me to his home in Los Angeles when his meetings concluded. We would visit with his family, and then return to Victoria by bus. His kind and generous invitation was accepted.

The three of us arrived in Los Angeles on Good Friday and met his family at their church in Hollywood. We had a happy and restful time with the Billesters and fully enjoyed their kind hospitality, the warm sunshine, and the relaxed atmosphere. When the time came to leave, Margarette and I got on the bus, crowded with servicemen, and said goodbye to the blue skies and tall palm trees. We would have good memories to look back on once we resumed our duties back at 2024.

Romance in the Hospital

Aunt Mildred was hospitalized in 1943 with undulant fever, caused by drinking raw milk. One day, Margarette said to one of the airmen, "Milton, why don't you take this book to Millie in the hospital?" Milton was deep into a book, sitting in a comfortable chair, and really didn't want to be disturbed. Margarette again said to him, "Milton, I think you should take this book to Millie." Resigned to doing as she asked, he walked the few blocks to the hospital. When he delivered the book to her room, he saw a pretty young woman sitting in bed.

That was the beginning of their romance. A navy man was also interested in her. One of the men would visit her, and as soon as he left, the other would show up at her room. Milton's Irish humor and dark good looks won out over the sailor, and they soon became engaged.

Milton was assigned to an air base in Alaska, but the two continued to make plans for their wedding. During the war, a wedding to a serviceman had to be approved by the commanding officer. Millie had to provide three letters of character recommendation. The required letters were sent, and the couple received approval to proceed with the marriage.

The date was set for early November. The couple chose a local church for the ceremony and made plans to have the reception at the Wills's home. Percy, a licensed minister, would perform the ceremony. Margarette began the task of providing food for the reception. Someone else provided the wedding cake, which in Canada is typically a dark fruitcake topped with almond paste and hard white icing.

Because sugar, eggs, butter, cream and other food staples were strictly rationed, Margarette began to hoard the items she would need in order to have a nice selection of goodies for the reception. Extra rations were available because they were feeding servicemen and women, but Percy had to keep an account of the number of meals in order to qualify for the additional food.

Another concern was how to store the perishable food. Like most families, Percy and Margarette didn't own a refrigerator—they were expensive at that time—but had an icebox where milk, butter and eggs were kept. The upper compartment held a 25-pound block of ice, while the lower compartment held only a small amount of food. To solve this problem, they used a vented cupboard on the back porch as a cooler for more food storage.

Two days before the wedding was to take place, the doorbell rang and a telegram was handed to Percy. It said that Milton had been delayed by stormy weather. He would not arrive in time for the scheduled ceremony. All the wedding plans suddenly came to a halt. The uncertainty made things difficult; some of the members of the wedding party were servicemen who had arranged leave for the ceremony, and it was unclear if they could rearrange to have that time off. And what about the food that had been so carefully hoarded? How long could it be kept? Would it have to be eaten at once?

Another telegram arrived that said Milton could fly into Victoria just two days later. We were all relieved, and the pace of decorating and planning picked up again. The wedding attendants were able to get new leave granted. The arrangements fell into place, and all was soon ready for the nuptials.

Millie and Milton were married that November in 1943, in a union that has lasted for more than 60 years.

Another Health Crisis for Margarette

About two or three years after her heart attack, Margarette had another serious health issue. She developed thrombophlebitis in her leg. The possibility of a clot breaking off and going either to her heart, lungs or brain was quite real. When her doctor suggested a certain treatment, Percy disagreed with it and located another doctor who had more experience in treating this condition. It is unknown if the current blood thinning medications were available at that time or not.

Her new doctor put her to bed for several weeks and monitored her condition carefully. Once again, friends came to help out by taking over some of her duties. I was older and could assume more responsibilities to keep the household running smoothly so that we could continue to serve the people who counted on 2024 so much. The night of the doctor's visit, I went outside to wait for him. He arrived, but instead of going in the house immediately, we stood for 10 or 15 minutes watching a meteor shower. There was a constant rain of falling lights. Finally, we could not stand our stiff necks any longer and went inside.

Often on the weekends, all the cots and other sleeping spots were filled, which put a heavy load on the home's one bathroom. In talking about this problem with the men one morning, Percy said, "I can be ready, washed, shaved and dressed in five minutes." One of the sailors took up his challenge. He retorted, "If you can really do that, I'll take you and Mom Wills out to the Empress Hotel for dinner!" The gauntlet was down.

A dinner at the best hotel in Victoria was almost an unknown event for Margarette and Percy. On the specified night, the sailor said, "I'll wake you up at 6:00 A.M., and I'll time you to be sure that you are completely dressed and ready to go in five minutes."

The next morning, Percy was awakened at 6:00 and headed straight for the bathroom, which had been cleared for the event. He washed and shaved, went back to the bedroom to dress, and then presented himself to the sailor in just under the time limit. True to his word, the sailor made a reservation at the Empress Hotel for the three of them. Margarette and Percy thoroughly enjoyed their sumptuous dinner served in the inimitable style of that hotel.

Another health issue that Margarette had to deal with was arthritis, which she probably developed late in their stay at 2024. It attacked only her hands, and the joints of her fingers became quite painful and swollen. She tried several treatments until she learned about the injections of gold salts. Some arthritic patients had benefited from this treatment, so Percy and Margarette decided to have the injections. It did stop the pain and the advance of joint swelling, but her knuckles never returned to normal. However, in spite of the disfigurement, her fingers remained nimble enough for her to continue her secretarial work. She was the only woman I knew who could type at her normal speed and carry on a conversation at the same time. Her speed and accuracy were amazing.

God Provides Food for Many

Procuring enough food to feed as many as 25 people at a meal was a great concern to Percy and Margarette. Prayer was their first recourse, and God was always faithful. Sometimes a farmer brought some meat or vegetables. Other times, a monetary gift came in the mail. One visiting soldier came from a family who had an interest in a major tea and coffee company, and he wrote home about their need. Not long after, a large package arrived containing pounds of tea, coffee and other items. It was a surprise that was received with thanks as another example of God's provision.

Left to right: Frank, Margarette, Percy and Darda Wills

One memorable time, the well-known catch of fish as recorded in Scripture repeated itself. Frank was coming home on leave and was bringing a friend with him. Because his son loved to fish and they needed meat for the meals, Percy decided to plan a fishing trip.

A friend in the city of Nanaimo owned a fishing boat, so Percy phoned him and asked if he would take him, Frank, and Frank's friend out to catch some salmon. The boat owner told him, "Oh, Percy, no one has caught any salmon up here in the last several days." Percy wanted to go anyway, and so the man agreed.

A day or two later, the three men, Margarette and I drove to the friend's home in Nanaimo. The men boarded the boat and went to fish. Percy and Margarette had been praying about the need and trusted God to supply it. It was not long until the salmon began taking the bait. Fish after fish was hauled on board until the hold was full.

Back home, the beautiful large salmon filled the laundry tubs. The men cleaned the fish, and then the women cut them up and packed them in jars for the pressure cooker. The tiring process took all day, but we were joyful and praised God for this miracle of His provision. Those jars of salmon enhanced our meals for quite awhile, especially for the people from the Prairie Provinces, who seldom had fresh salmon at a meal.

A Miracle Christmas

It was the very last Christmas holiday we would have at the big old house on Belmont Avenue. In one way it was sad, because we knew we probably would not see some of these wonderful servicemen and women again. We expected to have 25 people for the New Year's Day feast. The menu included a large roast beef with mashed potatoes, good brown gravy, vegetables and dessert.

The day before the holiday, Percy and Margarette were in the kitchen preparing the vegetables and setting the tables when the doorbell rang. When Percy opened the door, a large paper sack was thrust into his hands. It contained a huge turkey, which someone had sent as a surprise. Percy took it into the kitchen and showed it to Margarette. They wondered who had sent it and, more than that, what God was up to.

Just then the phone rang, and Percy and Margarette soon received their answer. Some China Inland Missionaries who had recently been released from a Japanese prison camp were on board an old tramp steamer that had anchored off shore. It was so derelict that it was a wonder it had made the journey across the Pacific Ocean and was still afloat. The crew had gone ashore for the holiday, but the missionaries were left alone on board. The caller wanted to know if Percy could do something for them.

Percy said that he would. Immediately, he called the immigration authorities, some of whom he knew personally, to see what could be done to bring the group to Victoria for the day. He discussed the matter with the authorities and was given permission to bring the group to his home, as long as he agreed to be responsible to guard them and return them to the ship. Percy readily agreed, hung up the phone, and then made some other necessary calls.

One was to a friend who had a boat, and the two made arrangements to get the group from the steamer to the shore. The next call was for another driver to join Percy and pick up the people at the dock. The distance was not far, but gas was strictly rationed. With those critical arrangements made, Percy and Margarette hurriedly began to prepare more vegetables, get the turkey ready for roasting, and set more tables in the big dining room. Now the guests numbered 41, not 25.

When the missionary group walked into our home the next day, the atmosphere was electric. These were missionaries and their children who had paid a heavy price to serve the Lord in China. They had been captured and had spent four years in prison camp. Some of their group had died from the mistreatment, and the rest were malnourished and so thin that their clothes hung on their bodies. Every eye that welcomed them was wet with tears—tears of realization of the dangers and severe persecution they had suffered at the hands of their captors. Yet here they stood, freed at last and back on their own land.

The children had never seen an orange, a beef roast or a turkey! The adults had not seen such an abundance of food for as long as they could remember. They sat at the table wide-eyed with awe at the grace of God who had arranged for this time of fellowship with other godly people.

After grace was said, there was little conversation as the guests filled their plates with satisfying food that pleased both the eye and the palate. It did not take long for the dishes heaped with food to be emptied and filled again. When everyone was sated and the conversation began to flow, Percy asked the senior missionary to tell them of their experiences and of their trip across the ocean. The man rose and spoke haltingly of some of their deprivations and the loss of one of the fathers. His descriptions were painful to hear, but they taught us of the price some had paid to tell other nations about Jesus' love and salvation. The missionary recounted the instances of God's faithfulness to them in their dire circumstances and how He upheld them time and time again with His Word and comforting presence.

He then remembered a little book he carried in his pocket, reached in and pulled it out. As he flipped through it, he told of being in Hong Kong the night before they left China. He went to a pagoda on the crest of a hill, where he could look out over the city. His heart was breaking for the people he had learned to love, and he prayed earnestly for the land he had to leave and its unknown future. He said that as he looked around the inside walls of the pagoda, he noticed some English names with Scripture references written beneath them. He read those names aloud.

Suddenly, someone gasped. A stunned silence fell over the room, and all eyes quickly turned to a couple of men sitting at the table. The missionary looked and wondered at the charged atmosphere. The two men stood. They were the ones who had written their names and those Scripture verses on that very wall in Hong Kong!

One of the other servicemen took Percy aside and asked if he could take up a collection for these missionaries. "Certainly, go to it!" Percy said. It didn't take long to gather a nice amount of money, which was then handed to the awed missionary. Word got out to others about this amazing event, and people began to bring gifts and other needed items to the house. One Christian man who owned a shoe store opened it up and fitted every one of them with new shoes.

That amazing day had yet one more emotional moment, for the daughter of one of the missionaries was a nurse in Toronto. Despite the protestations of her parents, Percy decided to make a long-distance call to her. When he made the call, he learned that the daughter was a patient in the hospital where she worked. She had undergone serious brain surgery and was now in recovery. Someone brought a telephone to her room so she and her parents could talk. We could overhear their conversation and tearful sobs, and it affected each one of us. Once more eyes brimmed with unshed tears, but hearts were full of gratitude to God for having a part in such a wonderful day.

At the end of the day, Percy and his friend transported the missionaries back to the dock, where the boat took them back to the rusty steamer. Each one wondered if they would ever meet again this side of heaven. That momentous day was a fitting climax to Percy and Margarette's years of ministering to men and women from many walks of life whose lives had been interrupted by war.

CHAPTER TEN

AFTER THE WAR

I will instruct you and teach you in the way you should go:
I will guide you with My eye.
(Psalm 32:8)

B Y THE END of 1945 the war was coming to a close, and
Percy and Margarette knew that their home for the servicemen and women would not be needed much longer. The
two had given a lot of thought and prayer as to where they would
live next, but they had not yet said anything to me. They looked
at several lots and finally decided on one that seemed to be the
best choice.

One evening, the three of us drove to this lot, which was located
in another area of town. It was two blocks from the bus stop and up a
slight hill. The lot was in their price range, and as we walked around
it, Percy took measurements for a proposed medium-sized home.

As we were doing this, a couple walked by. Percy noted them,
but he assumed they belonged in the neighborhood. The next day,
he went to the real estate office to bid on the lot but found it had

already been sold. He wondered if the couple he saw the previous night were the buyers.

God Knows Best

Percy and Margarette were not disturbed, for they expected that God had a better plan for them. God did. A much better plan. An older couple, who were friends, knew that Percy was looking for a place to build a home and told him of a lot for sale near them. Percy and Margarette went to look at it and found the site to be superior to the previous one.

It was near a corner where the bus stopped, which was important because Margarette didn't drive and had to have a way to get to work when Percy was away. There was a little strip mall next door, which included a grocery store, a drug store and a little fish and chip shop. You could run up a tab for your purchases at the grocery and pay the bill at the end of the month. It was so convenient to have it practically next door, especially during the winter months. (In later years when my family came for our annual visit, we ate several lunches at this fish-and-chip shop. Frank also interned at the drug store before his senior year in the pharmacy program at the University of British Columbia.)

The couple who told Margarette and Percy about the lot offered to lend them the plans for their home so they could build one just like it. Their home had a nice floor plan of two bedrooms, a bathroom, a kitchen, a dining room, a living room and an entry hall. The attic could be (and was) converted into two extra bedrooms. The basement contained a separate area for the garage.

God provided the last thing necessary before they could build. Only a few houses away, around the corner, lived an experienced building contractor whom Percy knew. He agreed to build the house. Now Percy had the lot, the house plans and the contractor. The only items left to procure were the building materials.

That was a major concern. With the war coming to a close, the country was transitioning from a wartime economy to a peacetime one. Construction that had been held in abeyance by the lack of materials was now being started. The servicemen and women who were returning to civilian life wanted to build homes for their families. As a result, there were shortages in almost all building products. Lumber that was not prime grade and would formerly have been rejected was now being used in home construction. One friend who was building his home couldn't get plaster for the inside walls, so his solution was to use cement instead.

Percy and Margarette's contractor was able to gather the necessary materials that would be needed once the foundation was completed. But first, he had to have the lot prepared for digging out the basement. The ground was clay and quite rocky, and sometimes the rocks had to be blasted in order to clear the way for laying the foundation. Finally, the lot was ready for the cement to be poured.

During the construction of the house, servicemen were still coming to 2024, although in fewer numbers. The work was slowly winding down, and Percy was preparing for the final days and sending reports to the government agencies. At last, the time came for the new house to be ready for occupancy. I believe it was the first house that Percy and Margarette had ever owned together. They said a fond

Margarette Wills in their new home

goodbye to 2024, their home for six years, and with anticipation and some questions, they moved into their new home during the last week of December 1946.

I was in my senior year of high school by this time. Margarette and Percy now had to decide what they wanted to do in this next phase of their lives. They had been praying about God's direction for this change for some while. Neither was able to lead a quiet life with little activity. So, once they were settled and things were going smoothly, Percy rejoined the Shantymen's Association and Margarette decided to get a part-time job. She was hired as the secretary of the credit union for the provincial government employees. Now their lives took on a new direction and purpose.

Once Margarette was in her own home, she had time to indulge her creative side. She began to create small floral bouquets from various kinds of colored fish scales and small shells. In the evenings she would sit at the kitchen table with her supplies in front of her, and then with tweezers and glue would place the tiny shells and scales on a piece of black velvet. When completed, she had the pictures framed and gave them as gifts, which were treasured. Another craft she enjoyed was doing *petit-point* needlework on fine mesh. These, too, became works of art that were lovingly displayed by those who received them.

Another instance of Margarette making good use of her time was when the ironing basket was full. She got home from work about 5:00 P.M., and if Percy was not yet home, she would start supper. While it was cooking, she would fold a sheet, lay it on the table and began ironing. By the time everything was cooked, she had made quite a dent in the task.

Frank had been discharged from the Air Force and now joined us at home. He took advantage of the G.I. Bill (an educational assistance program for veterans started after World War II) to complete his college education. Percy and Margarette also had a boarder who augmented the family while Percy was away.

Margarette and Percy continued entertaining at their new home, though not as frequently as they had at the house on Belmont Avenue. Percy would look for people at church who were from out of town and insist that they come home for dinner. They hosted some of the Shantymen's committee meetings, always with some of Margarette's good baking served with the tea.

Friends from the neighborhood or the church or those from out of town were always welcomed into the peaceful warmth of their home. One day, a couple from the hospital, Dr. McPherson and her husband, were visiting while Margarette was at work. In a letter to me, she related that Percy made them comfortable in the living room and chatted for a bit. Then he excused himself and went into the kitchen. He returned to talk with them again for a little while, and then returned to the kitchen. Finally, he came back and announced, "If you don't like potatoes, corn, hamburger and ice cream, lunch is finished." I had heard that sort of announcement before, and it had the desired effect of getting people to the table quickly.

One winter day, Percy had been invited to speak at an evening meeting at a church up-island. He was an engaging speaker who loved to tell the great things God was doing on the field and how He miraculously provided for the needs. Margarette, another woman and I made the journey with him.

Following the meeting, which was well attended, Percy drove toward home. The night was beautiful, and the frosted trees sparkled with rime as the car lights shone on them. It looked like thousands of brilliants scattered all over the landscape. We approached the Malahat hill and began to climb, but the car could not make it over the icy road. We began to slide backward, stopping only when we reached the bottom of the hill.

We sat quietly for a few minutes, each of us wondering how we were going to spend the night in a cold car. Percy took charge and told us to wait in the car while he sought refuge for us. He was not the least bit agitated but walked purposefully across the road. He headed for a few houses that were off the highway. He seemed to know which one to approach, as the porch light went on in response to his knock. We watched him in the distance and saw him turn around after a few minutes and head back for the car.

When he reached the car, he told us to follow him to the home where we had been invited to spend the night. We were amazed that a total stranger would take in four people who were stranded. I wondered how my dad knew which house to approach, for it seemed to be the first one he went to. It was just another example of God's presence leading him.

We were welcomed in, and the other lady and I were shown to an unused and unheated guest room. We looked at the bed and decided to sleep in our clothing for added warmth. It took a while for the bed to release its chill, but we finally slept well.

The next morning, we thanked our hosts and headed for the car. When we got into the car, the engine started right up. The frost had thawed sufficiently, and we now had no trouble making it up and over the Malahat drive. We were so thankful to God for providing a warm home for us to spend a cold night, and the warm hearts of the couple who took four absolute strangers into their family. We prayed that God would bless them for their hospitality.

A New Ministry Partner

When Percy resumed the boat ministry, he was joined by Harold Peters, a man whom God had chosen and trained for this ministry. While Percy and Margarette were busy with the war work, Harold had continued the boat ministry in the *Messenger II*. He was well acquainted with the familiar waters of the west coast. In God's providence, he had handled ships as a quartermaster all along these same routes in his previous career.

Harold had started his maritime career with the Union Steamship Company. He had been assigned to one of their boats that plied the waters between Vancouver and Alaska and around the Queen Charlotte Islands. On an early voyage when the dreaded flu epidemic was at its height, two quartermasters on his ship became ill. In desperation, the captain brought Harold into the wheelhouse, where he was shown how to steer by compass during the blackness of the night. Harold learned quickly and proved to be cool and composed under pressure. This earned him the respect of the captain, and thus Harold began his career.

When Harold and Percy met in the 1940s, they formed a strong bond of friendship. Each had tremendous respect for the other. They were like close brothers in their love for God and their concern for the people on the west coast, who sorely needed the aid and comfort they could bring to them. Both men had a great sense of humor and were quite adept at one-liners. One or the other could be heard saying, "I'm going to retire on land and take up lighthouse keeping," or, "This food tastes 'musty'—I 'musty' have some more!" When asked if he would like a second helping of pie or cake, Percy would sometimes say, "Yes, please. Just give me a little piece about the size of a doorstep." Another favorite expression of his was "happy-lu-yah," said with a satisfied smile on his face. A quiet "Praise the Lord" was heard frequently.

Both Percy and Harold had an even temperament and a rock-solid faith in God's provision and direction in even the smallest details. This reliance on the Holy Spirit's leading kept them from danger several times. Their early morning devotional times were spent in prayer, reading from the Bible and meditating on the passage they had read. Frequently, one would begin to sing or whistle a hymn. Changes in schedule due to weather or problems that had developed or their immediate financial needs never changed their attitude of implicit trust. In fact, Percy would sometimes query someone by saying, "How do you think God is going to provide the large sum needed for this project?" He always wanted God to receive the glory for the answer when it came.

The two men worked together in great harmony. Each complemented the other in his desire that every person they met should know that Jesus loved them and would save them for eternity. They were assertive but not aggressive. They were loving and forthright in their presentation of the gospel, whether it was to one person, a family, a number of men in a bunkhouse, or a church group. Their purpose was to make sure people knew how good God was and how He provided miraculously for every need. Their joy was infectious and constant, regardless of their circumstances.

The staff at the hospital in Esperanza, which had been built on the west coast in 1937, was always eager to see the *Messenger II* (and later the *Messenger III*) heading for their dock. In preparation, they made sure there was plenty of hot water so Percy and Harold could each have a hot bath and do their laundry. Such pleasures could not be had on the boat and were much appreciated. Another great pleasure was the fellowship of the godly people who selflessly lived and worked in that place. The communion with like-minded people was spiritually refreshing to both men.

Percy and Harold became known for a culinary first. They had developed a sandwich on the boat, and it became a hit with the hospital staff. It consisted of a slice of orange on top of a slice of onion, which was then placed between two slices of homemade bread and liberally spread with butter and mayonnaise. It became known as "the Shantymen's sandwich." As the two men made these sandwiches, they chattered and joked between themselves and with the others in the kitchen enjoying the repartee.

One evening in 1948, Margarette and I were attending a Youth for Christ meeting in Victoria. During the meeting, an usher approached Margarette with the news that the *Messenger II* with Dr. McLean and his son, Bruce, on board had foundered on the rocks in a fierce storm near Esperanza inlet. Preliminary reports were not good. Attempts to contact Percy and Harold by radio on board

Messenger III were not getting through. They had no idea where they were, or if they too had suffered damage in the storm.

We hurriedly left the meeting and went home with heavy hearts, praying desperately for Percy, Harold and the McLean family. It was a long, wakeful night. Even though the missionaries and their wives knew the risks involved in being caught at sea in a full storm, they continued to trust that God would protect their loved ones in such times. Not one of the men was foolhardy. Never would they put out to sea if the weather were worsening, unless it was an emergency.

The next day, we learned that Dr. McLean had been rescued from his precarious perch on a rock but that his son, Bruce, was lost at sea. The full story is better told in Louise Johnson's book, *Not Without Hope*.

Margarette and I learned that Percy and Harold had been able to put into a sheltered cove, where they rode out the storm. The hills around them had blocked their radio reception. The next day, they learned the details of Dr. McLean's rescue and of the loss of Bruce and the boat.

The extent of the mission work had grown, and now there were summer camps and Daily Vacation Bible Schools (DVBS) for children. Children had to be transported by boat from their villages to the campsites. It was quite an undertaking to get the children on board and quieted prior to sailing.

While the adults who accompanied the children got them settled, Percy and Harold prepared the boat for the trip. They felt the heavy responsibility for the lives of those on board, and they committed every journey to the care of the loving Shepherd who watches over all His children. When the boat left the shelter of the bay, it had to make its way out into the Pacific Ocean. If the sea were choppy, it would be a tense, several-hour run to the camp, for there was no other way to go. On one trip, the waves were rolling in to shore and the motion made the children ill. It was a relief to all to finally arrive at the campsite and deliver the children safely. Once again, their trust in God's control of the weather was affirmed.

Another part of the mission work was the distribution of Bibles, New Testaments, Scripture portions, and tracts. The missionaries scattered the Scriptures in many places on the continent, as well as mailing Bibles and the Shantymen's newsletter out to many places on Earth. Bibles were placed in defense bases, jails, harbor offices, hospitals, and wherever they were asked to provide the gospel material.

But one of the sweetest experiences transpired at the great PNE (Pacific National Exhibition) in Vancouver, when a team of their missionaries gave out some 8,000 Gospels of John. Several times they went around the grounds, to see if the Gospels had been willfully thrown away amongst the litter that always attends the fair. Only one copy was found lying on the ground, and it was only there one minute before a little girl picked it up and cried out to her father who was coming along behind. "Look, Daddy, see what I have found!" As soon as the father had seen the beautiful SGM (Scripture Gift Mission) booklet, he said, "Isn't it beautiful! I wonder where we could get two more for your brothers?" Naturally, it was not long before the little girl's brothers were supplied as well.

(PW)

CHAPTER ELEVEN

THE CAMPS

You shall love the Lord your God with all your heart, with
all your soul, and with all your strength. And these words,
which I command you today, shall be in your heart. You
shall teach them diligently to your children, and shall
talk of them when you sit in your house, when you walk
by the way, when you lie down and when you rise up.
(Deuteronomy 6:5-7)

PERCY AND HAROLD, the skipper, had a great love for children, especially those on the west coast who knew nothing of play areas or community parks. Toys were simple items, often handmade. The teenagers had no places to "hang out," and few jobs were available to them. The lack of positive activities during the long, sunny days of summer were of real concern to both men. They both thought and prayed much about what could be done. Their prayers were answered in conjunction with the group at Nootka Mission Hospital.

In 1948, the mission hospital began a children's camp at Ferrier Point, which almost immediately was mispronounced "Ferrer" Point, and the name stuck. Donnel McLean was the director, and his brother, Bruce, at 14, was a helper. Three other assistants came from Prairie Bible Institute. One of the students, Earl Johnson, later became a Shantymen missionary and then, when Dr. McLean retired, became the superintendent of the Nootka Mission.

That first camp drew 32 campers for the 10-day period. It was so successful that parents questioned the leaders about what they had done for their children, because the kids raved so much about the camp. However, it was not until the third summer that camp was held again. In the meantime, several old buildings had to be razed, and the campground and main building had to be refurbished to prepare for the next group of children. It was a daunting task, and it looked as if the camp would not be able to continue. The hospital group prayed earnestly about this problem, for they believed that Ferrier Point was the best location. God answered their prayers by sending a team of students to do the backbreaking work of clearing and renovating.

When word went out that summer camp would begin, children came from all over the coast. Boys and girls came from Port Hardy, Coal Harbor, Kyuquot, Hot Springs Cove, Ahousat, Tofino and Port Alberni. There were no roads connecting these places, so all the campers had to be brought by boat through the dangerous open water.[1]

The sea was very rough on that first trip. Many of the children were sitting in the stern seasick and throwing up continuously. I was fearful that someone might become so weak he might even fall overboard.

My imagination and helplessness got the better of me. I went down into the hot engine room, took hold of the railing around the engine, and prayed. It turned out to be not as long a prayer as I expected. I did not know exactly what to pray. All I said was, "Oh, Lord, please give me your peace." And He did.

(PW)

The shipload of children arrived safely. Children recover quickly, and once they got on land, they ran about checking out the tents, the play area, the kitchen and everything. They found it all good and exciting.

Every year that camp was held, all the equipment and supplies had to be ferried across the open seas to Camp Ferrier, about 21 miles from the hospital grounds. Once at the camp location, everything had to be barged to the beach. The tides and large breakers precluded the building of a wharf or float.[2]

This camp continued for another 12 or 13 years, during which time hundreds of children heard the gospel story of Jesus and His love. It was also a training ground for Bible School students, who were recruited for the summer's work. The primary purpose of the summer camps was not just to introduce the children to the camping experience but also to give them the knowledge of their importance to God and His love for each of them. Surrounded by God's creation and the loving ministrations of the young leaders, the children were taught Bible stories and learned the choruses that spoke of Jesus.

The missionaries, leaders, and counselors at camp were wise enough not to push the children to accept Jesus as their Savior before the end of camp. Such hurried decisions often do not last. Instead, the leaders prayed for the children and allowed the Holy Spirit to do His tender work of drawing each child to Himself in God's time.

Percy was able to bring Christian teens to be leaders in the camp and hold DVBS classes in some of the villages. In order to secure enough volunteer teachers, he contacted Multnomah School of the Bible in Portland, Oregon; Three Hills Bible College in Alberta, Canada; and Biola in Los Angeles, California. The schools made these opportunities available to the students as short-term mission work. Volunteers spent their summer vacations teaching children in this out-of-the-way area. Percy and the prayer group in Victoria prayed earnestly for the Lord to send only those young people who would fit in best with the primitive conditions.

Those who volunteered found a mission field only a few hundred miles from their urban locations. For the students who were considering a missions career, teaching DVBS in the coastal villages was a prime opportunity for them to get a feel for a life of ministering in under-developed countries overseas. Some of the volunteers came for two or three summers, and some dedicated themselves to God for a life of service in other lands.

A Fragrant Talk at Church

Years later, during the time that some of the Biola students taught DVBS on the coast, Percy was invited to speak at the New Year's Eve service held at the Church of the Open Door in Los Angeles. This church was the site of the Biola campus at that time. My husband and I lived a few miles east of Los Angeles, and we looked forward to having my dad and mother stay with us. Our boys were excited that "Nana" and "Bumpa" would be there just after Christmas.

During supper the night before he was to speak, Percy reached for the little shaker of dried garlic chips on the table. He was a great cook and knew how to season things well, and he particularly liked garlic. He took the lid off the bottle, not realizing there was no shaker part on it. As he shook the jar, several spoonfuls of garlic chips landed on his meat. We all gasped and suggested he scrape most of it off the dish, but he declined. He didn't realize the potency of the dried garlic.

The next evening, he and Margarette drove to Los Angeles. The air inside the car was fragrant with the odor of the herb. When we arrived, we found seats in the audience, but he went immediately to the platform. He spoke to the men assembled there and apologized to them. He said that he had bathed, then showered, and then tried everything he could to minimize the odor, but nothing worked.

The garlic had got into his pores and could not be disguised by any means.

That incident became a big family joke every time he bought some garlic sausage and offered a slice of it to us.

Expanding the Campsites

The number of campers at Ferrier Point increased year after year. The logistics and safety concerns involved with rounding up and delivering the many children by boat in a timely manner began to raise the question as to whether there was a better way to serve the needs of the children up and down the coast. A new plan had to be developed.

God had been gracious in watching over the transportation of the hundreds of campers so that not one accident took place. On the other hand, the missionaries felt the need to reduce the time spent out on the open sea. After considerable prayer, thought and deliberation, it was decided to start two more campsites.

The first one, Camp Ross, was at Pachena Bay and would serve the southern part of the island in the Barkley Sound area. The second one was Camp Henderson in Quatsino Sound, which would serve the northern sector of the coast. The central area was served by Ferrier Point camp. Although the children still had to be ferried to the camps, the waterways were sheltered in the sounds. There was no need to take the children out on the open sea, which increased the safety factor. The running time for each trip was shortened, which meant that more children could be accommodated.

Over the years, hundreds of children spent a week each summer at one of the camps. Not only were the children affected by the gospel that was clearly and lovingly presented, but the parents also saw the effects of God's work in their children. It was a witness to them of the love and mercy of God, and it opened them up to the witness of the missionaries as well.

In 1958, a shortage of funds developed during the fall season. Percy writes of it this way:

As a result of these many experiences [of God's timely provision], there has been built up a hope that makes the committee unashamed as they approach the new and varied problems ahead. So it has become a habit to call for a Day of Prayer in each extremity.

One of the most recent was during the fall season, when the treasury had been drained by the heavy summer programs. Our missionaries were needing finances for their families, but there was no help in the treasury. The final Thursday of the month arrived, and no help in sight. The luncheon at the YWCA was alerted, as the field force joined with the committee for a day of prayer. The following Monday, being the first Monday of the next month, was the regular business meeting of the committee. On the way to the meeting, our secretary was handed a letter which enclosed a check for five thousand dollars. One paragraph in the letter was most revealing, "Dear friends of the Shantymen—I feel strangely moved to send you the enclosed check for your work, and trust that it will be sufficient."

The writer knew nothing of the needs of the Society, but hearing the voice of the Lord she had responded to His call.

(PW)

CHAPTER TWELVE

MENTOR TO THE YOUNGER MISSIONARIES

*You therefore, my son, be strong in the grace that is in
Christ Jesus. And the things that you have heard from
me among many witnesses, commit these to faithful men who will be able to teach others also.*
(2 Timothy 2:1-2)

E VERY MISSION ORGANIZATION needs an influx of younger
people who can bring their God-given talents to the group.
The older missionaries must transfer their responsibilities
to the younger ones while working alongside one another. The
first ones on the field will need to step back and allow the second
generation of workers to move ahead and bring the changes in
method—but not in the message—that will be needed.

Percy and Harold had spent long years on the sea. They were
still strong physically, but it was time to inculcate those just joining
the mission with the ways of God as they were played out in daily
life. That meant teaching them to rely totally on God for every
need, be it financial, physical or spiritual. That lesson was not easily
learned—especially when the petty cash box was empty and the

boat had to be fueled and provisioned before leaving port just when the tide was right—but by working with those who knew the ways of God, it could be done. It was not uncommon to have the supply trucks leave the dock just as someone came with money to pay the bills. Both Percy and Harold walked closely with God and were led daily by the Spirit. They expected God to provide for them.

Instructing the next generation of missionaries also meant teaching them to serve the people to whom they wanted to minister. Serving came first; then the witness by words. Each person was important in the eyes of God, regardless of his or her ethnicity, background, education or lack of it. Each one had an eternal soul for whom Christ died. The younger missionaries needed to be taught by the example of the two seasoned men, and no opportunity for service was passed by or considered demeaning. With learning, the new missionaries found it to be a joyous way to live, for it showed the heart of God in ways words could not.

The new missionaries also had to learn how to live together in the close quarters of the ship. The mission could not be jeopardized by personality conflicts on board. Percy has been quoted as praying, "Dear Lord, send us good men, but no misfits, please." He knew the Holy Spirit was grieved when His children doing His assigned work could not get along in unity of purpose.

There were other lessons for the new missionaries to learn while working with Percy and Harold, but the above three were the most important. Each man who came aboard, whether for a short term or for a lifetime, was blessed to be mentored by these seasoned, godly men.

Percy and Harold were highly respected, even by those who were in opposition to their message. Another of Percy's quotes is, "Enemies make wonderful friends once they've been converted." The believers loved each of these two with a deep emotion, and no one was more welcomed in their homes than they were. Faces lit up when the *Messenger III* pulled up to the dock and Harold and Percy stepped onshore.

> Each visit was full of caring assistance, however it was needed. People were encouraged and uplifted by the gentle, happy spirit exhibited. The children ran to us, sat on our laps, and insisted we play games or tell them stories. They also listened while the children told Harold and me their secrets or showed us their simple toys. Adults found us easy to confide in and were comforted with the Scriptures and our prayers.
>
> (PW)

The new missionaries learned some of these lessons almost by osmosis. Both Harold and Percy knew how to mentor and encourage the younger men. They had the ability to see the potential of the recruits and draw out their gifts. Each young person they trained

Left to right: Harold Peters, Donnel McLean, Percy Wills

was given assignments to develop and exercise those gifts. In serving, the younger people had to move quickly when they saw a need, or Percy would already be tending to it. The example was worth hundreds of words in teaching the lesson.

One of the young missionaries, Donnel McLean, a son of Dr. and Mrs. McLean, had grown up on the west coast of Vancouver Island. As a teenager, he was involved in the camp program as a director. Donnel lived with Percy and Margarette for a while and then joined Percy on board the *Messenger III*. He recently sent me a page of his memoirs of "Uncle Perc," as he called him. One example he gives of Percy's heart for the lonely people in his mission field is as follows:

> One memorable time it was my privilege to go with him on one of the ventures. Our goal? An isolated, lonely lighthouse where lived some very lonely folk. After hiking through a narrow trail of an hour or two we visited those precious lonely lighthouse keepers, always sharing the good news and closing with prayer. But on our return to a small channel area that was easily crossable earlier, to our dismay the tide had come in, cutting our return off. Nonchalantly Percy and I gathered together some mini logs with which we came up with a small raft, but, of course, there were no nails or wires holding it together. Getting on board about midway our "raft" came apart and into the cold, wintry fall waters we fell, getting all wet and chilled to the bone. Can you see the two of us, wet to the gills, trudging along singing songs? That was Percy! What an example of Christ he always was to me. Always!

Another example he gives of Percy's servant heart with its message of love, joy, and wondrous hope is this one:

> Percy would leave his [boat] and head off into the woods following trails and paths. Finding a home he would knock on

the door and find a lonely little mother holding, perhaps, a baby with another toddler at her feet. Dirty dishes were piled high, the wood box was empty and the fire was going out. Immediately, while whistling a gospel tune, Percy would head outside, cut a stack of wood, carry it into the house and fill the wood box and, of course, stoke up the fire so the house would get all cozy and warm. Then without a word he would cheerfully go to the dishpan and wash all the dirty dishes and, finally, then he would encourage the weary little mother to sit down and listen. Can you begin to imagine how eagerly that soul would listen or how deeply the Shantyman missionary's prayer would bless her? Oh, how loved was this beloved "missionary."

Donnel also told me of the times Percy would talk with him personally and say, "I don't know why I'm telling you this . . . " and then go on to relate something he had experienced during his years on the field. Percy did not talk about people who may have opposed his work or betrayed him or even tell of things done behind his back. I don't recall ever hearing a critical comment about anyone or his allowing gossip to be spoken. He would never tell us of the great work he was doing. It was always the great things God was doing: how individuals were getting saved or delivered from bondage, or how God was miraculously providing funds for some need at the time.

After a year or two with the Shantymen, Donnel left to further his missionary training. There he met his wife, Venda. After their marriage they went to Japan, where they ministered until their retirement.

Harold's Invitation

Another young man, Earl Johnson, who later joined the mission, lived in the town of Port Alberni. While there, he became acquainted with the Shantymen. When it came time for him to go to high school, he was sent to the boarding school at Three Hills, Alberta. During his time at the school, he dedicated himself completely to God for service. He wanted to go to China, but the communist takeover there precluded that possibility.

Earl's summers were spent working in the sawmills on the coast, earning money to pay for his schooling. He still found time to witness, and in following summers he worked among the youth in the valley. He was very concerned for their spiritual welfare, as so few of them knew of God or Christ's love for them, even though there were churches in town.

One day, Earl met Harold and saw in him a godly character, a strong personality and complete dedication to his mission. Harold made a deep impression on Earl. When they met the second time, Harold asked Earl if he would like to come on board the *Messenger III* and be a deck hand. Earl was surprised at the offer, for he barely knew Harold. But he said he would take the time to consider it. When they next met, Earl told Harold that he could not join him at that time, as he was committed to the group of young people with whom he had been working.

But God was in the meeting of the two. When Earl went back to Bible School and gave more consideration to Harold's invitation, God made it clear to him that this was the mission field he was being prepared for, not China. When he submitted his application to the Shantymen to work on the *Messenger III*, he was accepted. Right after his graduation, he joined the crew and began his training under the eye of Harold. There were all the workings of the boat to learn, the nautical ways of the sea, how to handle the ship in both quiet and stormy waters, and on and on. Earl was an adept pupil and learned rapidly and thoroughly the lessons Harold taught him.

Once more, God had provided just the right man at the right time. While Donnel left the Shantymen to eventually go to Japan, Earl stayed on for the next 16 years. He worked seamlessly with both Percy and Harold. The three were one in spirit and desire to see that every person they met, no matter how casually, received some witness of God's love and saving grace. In 1968, Earl sensed a need for graduate studies in counseling and enrolled in Seattle Pacific College and the University of Washington.

Some of the trainees in the late 1940s and 1950s were women, who were also impacted and impressed by the Christlike life of Percy. Most of the young women were busy with the camp programs during the summer.

Nurses had come to the hospital since the time it opened and, as the hospital expanded, so did the complement of nurses. God also provided other doctors to complement Dr. McLean's work at Esperanza. They, too, learned the ways of ministering to all the inhabitants of the west coast by accompanying Dr. McLean on his rounds of the villages.

CHAPTER THIRTEEN

THE *MESSENGER III* IS BUILT

When you pass through the waters, I will be with you; and through
the rivers, they shall not overflow you. When you walk through
the fire, you shall not be burned, nor shall the flame scorch you.
For I am the LORD your God, the Holy One of Israel, your Savior.
(Isaiah 43:2-3)

THE INCREASE IN young personnel added to the demands made on the *Messenger II*. Percy and Harold felt the time had come to build a bigger and faster boat that could meet the demands of the increased load. They prayed for God to make His will known and then presented this matter to the committee for prayer.

As the committee prayed for direction in the matter, the consensus came that they should go forward and build a boat to be named *Messenger III*. The decision was made in spite of the knowledge that adequate funds were not on hand for such an expensive undertaking. The committee added this need to their prayers and asked God to provide the funding for this boat, as He had done for the previous one.

After the decision was made to go forward, inquiries were made to the local shipyards about the type of vessel that would meet their needs, the approximate cost, and how soon the ship could be completed. In this instance, God had gone ahead of them and prepared the way. One of the shipyards in Victoria had just completed a 40-foot troller for a commercial fisherman. The hull was well designed, and the structure was sturdy enough to take the pounding of the treacherous waters in which it would sail. As Percy and Harold looked over the plans, they believed this type of ship would best fit their needs. The necessary modifications to the superstructure would not be a major problem, and as an added bonus, the plans were already drawn and made available for their use. A further consideration was that the builders were familiar with the construction, so the project could proceed quickly. With all this information in hand, the decision was made to go ahead and build this type of boat.

The builder told the committee that the cost to get the ship completed and ready to sail would be between 14,000 to 15,000 dollars. If only the hull and superstructure were built, without engines or fittings, the cost would be between 9,000 to 10,000 dollars. But even with the lower figure, there was still no money in the mission treasury.

As these deliberations were going on, Percy was in Toronto at the Shantymen's head office. The day before he was to return home, he had lunch with two businessmen he knew. During the conversation about the Vancouver Island work, they told him they wanted to contribute to the boat fund. They had been praying for the work, but now they wanted to do more. Each man took out his checkbook and promptly wrote a check for 2,500 dollars. Percy was astounded. As he looked at the checks, he realized that God had just provided 5,000 dollars, almost half of the necessary amount. His heart was full of praise and thankfulness for this timely gift, and it indicated to him that God was giving His approval to the new venture.

Percy asked the men to forward their checks to the committee in Victoria, as he knew it would be a great encouragement to them and the weekly prayer group to know that the funds were available to begin building. On the strength of this donation, and in faith that God would provide the rest of the money, orders were given to the builders to start construction. However, in the new post-war economy, all contracts were being written as cost-plus, because the prices of most building supplies rose frequently. This was not just for the lumber; the prices of the various metals required for shipbuilding also continued to climb. Only the best materials could be used in building the *Messenger III*, regardless of their price, because of the heavy weather forces to which the boat would be subjected. This was yet another reason for Percy and the prayer group to petition God for the overall funding of the construction. In many ways, God did provide every single need throughout the time the boat was being built, until it finally was commissioned.

The committee requested that the builder give them a week-by-week report on the costs incurred. It was the practice of the Shantymen that, as Christians, they should not incur any debt beyond the usual 30-day credit period. They were well aware that this debt could quickly climb over that limit because of the rapidly rising cost of materials.

The day came when the builders gave the committee the news that their estimate of 9,000 to 10,000 dollars had been reached. Only the hull and the part of the superstructure containing the wheelhouse and cabin had been completed. All the money that had been donated for the boat account had been used. As the committee considered the matter, they realized the final cost could grow to more than 20,000 dollars. So they decided to launch the hull as it was and not allow such a debt to be incurred.

Putting Hands to the Task

The *Messenger II* was brought around to tow the hull from Victoria north to Nanaimo where it was to be berthed. Percy and Harold took on the daunting task of doing what they could with their own hands and skill to complete the work on the superstructure. Friends also came to volunteer in any way they could. If God could give the Hebrew builders of the Tabernacle in Moses' day the necessary talent to build those structures never before seen and overlay them with gold, He could certainly give the needed skill to the hands of the faithful believers working on the vessel He had commissioned.

So it was that, little by little, the boat began to take its intended shape. I'm sure, knowing the character of the two men, that they prayed, praised, whistled and sang as they worked carefully and diligently alongside the friends who were giving their time. This was a ship that would bring the gospel to many people and would also bring glory to God. No effort was spared, no difficulty was too hard, no hours were too long for them. The newest navigational equipment was ordered for the pilothouse. They were doing all this for the Lord, and He would reward them for their industry.

An unusual and interesting way that God took care of one important need is told in the book *Splendour from the Sea*.[1] When it came time for the electrical wiring to be done, the man who was head of the local electrical firm became more and more enthusiastic about the project. He spent many extra hours night after night working on the installations. His wife accompanied him to make a pot of tea and lend a hand wherever she could help.

When the work was completed, the man was asked to present his bill. "Bill?" he shouted. "I should say there will be no bill! The pleasure has been mine. My wife and I have been church members all our lives, we have sung in choirs and all that, but this is the only and first time we have discovered for ourselves the utter joy of life—real life in Christ—and serving His cause! If you wish to repay us, then allow us to go on a little cruise with you in your work for a few days."

Those "few days" became eight months of service and help to the Shanty boys. Wherever the boat went, in good weather and bad, the musical talents of the electrician and his wife were a blessing to those in the meetings or on board. Their good humor and laughter were sorely missed when they had to return to their home. As an added blessing to the wife, her general health and strength increased due to her time spent at sea.

Another time while the boat was still under construction, a bill for 2,000 dollars for fittings and equipment became due and had to be settled. Percy was particularly burdened for this need, for there was no money in the bank to pay it. He continued in prayer as he left home early on a Monday morning, submitting this pressing need to God.

I have a clear memory of that bright and sunny day. Margarette and I were working in the kitchen when a man knocked on the back door. He was a local farmer, and he told Margarette that the Lord had spoken to him while he was driving his tractor and told him to go to his bank in Victoria, withdraw 2,000 dollars and take it to the missionary. He immediately complied, came to our house, and handed Margarette two 1,000-dollar savings bonds, half of which was to go to the building project and half to the hospital at Esperanza. She expressed her gratitude and said she would call Percy to let him know of his gift. God's timing and the knowledge that the farmer, who was in his middle years, had taken funds from his retirement money in obedience to God's leading awed us both.

When Margarette talked to Percy that evening, she passed on to him the farmer's wishes for the division of his gift. Percy, too, was so grateful to pass along the news of another measure of God's faithful watch over His work. The constant, timely provision of God by different means always built faith in the hearts of the committee and others who heard of it.

Messenger III

When the *Messenger III* was finally completed in 1949, she was docked at the wharf in the inner harbor in Victoria. It was the same place where the *Messenger II* had been dedicated in 1934. Her dedication service was unique, in that two other mission boats tied up at the same wharf were dedicated on the same day. A couple of unidentified newspaper clippings tell about the event, one of which, dated Friday, July 22, 1949, read as follows:

A dedication service for three medical-mission boats—two Canadian and one American—will be held in the Inner Harbor in front of the Parliament buildings Sunday evening.

The service is unique in that it is seldom that craft engaged in this work are in the same locality at one time.

The three boats are the 135-foot *Willis Shank*, converted U.S. Navy minesweeper of the Marine Medical Mission, Seattle; the

Bruce McLean, speedy new craft of the Nootka Hospital, and the *Messenger III* of the Shantymen's Christian Association.

There are stories behind the names of two of the ships. The *Willis Shank* is named after a Seattle Youth for Christ leader who was killed in a plane crash while flying to Alaska to dedicate a new mission, and the *Bruce McLean* is named for the fifteen-year-old son of Dr. H. A. McLean, who was drowned when the *Messenger II* was wrecked on the reefs near Tatchu Point on the west coast of the island on Oct. 2, last year.

One of the news items noted that about 1,500 people lined the embankment by the Parliament buildings to watch the proceedings. The three skippers were Captain C. Stabbert of the *Willis Shank*, Harold Peters of the *Messenger III*, and Percy Wills, looking after the *Bruce McLean* at that time. The article stated that the *Willis Shank* was en route to Alaska to visit isolated points with medical and spiritual aid.

Providence at Sea

Percy relates an event after the *Messenger III* was commissioned when God provided just the right person at the right time in a small out-of-the-way village:

> A couple of years later, the *Messenger III* was approaching the narrow inlet on her run from one [First Nations] village to another. The channel was narrow and tortuous, studded with many a ragged reef. Night was drawing on quickly and the winter air was filled with snow flurries. However, in the pilothouse all was warm and snug, and no concern was felt over the poor visibility for the radar screen was beautifully clear.
>
> Suddenly the image was cut from the screen and everything was dark. Immediately there was consternation and confusion. Men were sent to the forepeak and mast, but visibility had closed

to zero. Fearfully they felt their way along, and at last reached their destination.

The following morning the crew prepared to leave for another port but hesitated running the dangerous channel again, for the snow was falling fast. Such conditions at sea are always hazardous. As they were due to conduct services at their next point that morning, they prayed to God for help. How could God help in such an impossible circumstance, far from scientific help?

They had no sooner risen from prayer than a man came aboard saying that he was a technician sent in to fix the radar on a large tug. His plane was storm-bound for two days and he wanted some company. When he heard of our plight, he immediately asked for permission to see the set. In half an hour the radar was performing perfectly once more and we were on our way for the Lord. Had we been forced to send for such service the cost would have been prohibitive and the delay extensive.

(PW)

In February 1958, a storm packing 100-mile gale force winds struck the Zeballos Marine base, causing heavy damage. This is one example of severe winter storms to which the *Messenger III* was subject. A man by the name of Amos Zehr was on board the *Messenger III* and described the event:

We were on a routine cruise with the *Messenger III* and her crew as we came off the Pacific and ran into the Esperanza Inlet and up to the Mission Hospital at Ceepeecee. I was to take the plane from that point on my way home to Fort Wayne, Indiana, but I did not leave for another day when the storm had blown itself out. But that trip I shall never forget, not for the seas and the winds primarily, but for the great gang of men and women who labor on the lonely stretch of the Pacific Ocean, taking the gospel to the men and women who live on its shores.

During a three-week trip, in spite of tremendous rains and storms, the *Messenger III* and her crew took me to place after place where they very seldom saw a missionary, and some of them saw much of hardship and danger. Both to the Christians, who were hungry for fellowship, and to the non-Christians who have learned to love the fifty-foot craft, the "*Messenger*" is known as the "*Messy-boat*." Several times the groups would come down to wave us on our way after our services were concluded and we were forced to go on our journey to other points.

May I give you a little résumé of that journey? We averaged over one service per day, in spite of very bad weather and pouring rain. We traveled many hundreds of miles by sea, and some of them were boisterous. Some of the waters navigated were through reef-strewn channels hardly wider than the boat herself. But it was to the crew that my attention was strangely drawn; the skipper, Harold Peters, well loved and capable of handling his boat under any conditions; the mate, Rev. Earl Johnson, already sitting for his master's ticket (a seamanship ticket for a three hundred and fifty ton vessel in Canadian waters), and his wife, Louise, a registered nurse with one sweet daughter and now expecting another child in the near future. The engineer [was] Wilber James, graduate of seminary training and as full of vim as a young man can be. His wife, Barbara, a registered nurse as well, and newly come to the coast from her home in Michigan, where she had led a sheltered life in a country town.

In one district, we met a Christian family who were so hungry for fellowship that they were desperate. Peculiarly, we were stormbound there for one day, and what a day that was! It was full of the glory and the presence of the Lord, until our hearts overflowed with the beauty and blessing of God. Was it any wonder that we were all openly weeping when we said good-bye, at last?

Percy writes of the happiness of being a missionary and delightful hours spent in easy relaxation at the end of the long, busy days:

The boat called at Namu one stormy night, and a crowd of fishermen came aboard for a "muggup." After the service there was music and food. In the hearty atmosphere reserves were quickly broken down and confidences were shared. As the fellows were leaving to go aboard their own craft for the night, an Englishman said, "I've always had a rather different impression of missionaries. I have never gone to church, for I always thought that you fellows were sort of gaunt and earnest; but I have a very different feeling now."

From the grit and grime of daily life amongst the trucks, cars, boats, etc., have evolved such sayings as these:

"The belt came off the boiler and we began to sink."
"It must have been something I et."
"One more crust and I shall bust."
"Carry I out, but don't bend I."

These and a thousand other sayings have joined the ranks of the Shanty Boys. Even in connection with the work itself, how often the inner chuckle is so close to the surface. For instance, at the close of a wedding service [which I conducted] I asked the groom to salute the bride. Having no knowledge of any other than a military salute, the man obligingly turned to face the bride, clicked his heels together and smartly brought his right hand to his forehead.

(PW)

The *Messenger III* continued her routine calls on both the west coast and eastern waterways of Vancouver Island for the next decade. The ports of call ranged north to the Queen Charlotte Islands and into southern Alaska. But in 1960, her engines, which had performed well for 13 years, let it be known that they were near the end of their useful existence. According to Percy's record of this time, the replacement of the engines happened like this:

One of the most recent revelations of the temporal care which God lavishes on His children concerned the *Messenger III*. When the Shantymen built her in 1946, they had used the best materials and made her especially strong for the battle on the Pacific Coast. However, as diesel engines were then at a premium, a temporary installation was put in the engine room until such times as a better unit could be procured. That temporary unit worked, and worked hard, for thirteen years. At the end of that time . . . the unit began to collapse and a replacement was urgently needed.

It was admitted that the need must be met and action should be taken. A special meeting [of the committee] was called and a contract entered into for a seven thousand dollar installation job. Where would such wealth of money come from, over and above the ordinary operating costs? Prayer was made, and the matter laid on the broad shoulders of our wonderful Lord.

That very morning, unknown to the committee, a man had walked into our office and laid down a check for five thousand dollars. He knew nothing of our needs but his sister had passed to be with the Lord, and had expressed the desire that he would give that amount to the Shantymen. After the decision of the committee was made, and the contract sealed, the check was produced. How we all rejoiced and praised God!

Why had the Lord withheld that check for so long and pro-duced it at that particular moment? The woman had passed away months before; her will had specified clearly the above amount; but the money had not been forthcoming until the committee had made their decision. It arrived just a few hours before they signed the contract, although they were unaware of its coming. The Lord had accomplished His purpose in His usual delightful way. Before we had called, He had already answered.

(PW)

CHAPTER FOURTEEN

AIDING NEW WORKS

*Besides the other things, what comes upon me daily: my deep
concern for all the churches.*
(2 Corinthians 11:28)

E
VEN BEFORE PERCY retired, he had established new works
or consulted with others who had a dream to begin a new
kind of work. Both the Stranger's Rest in Port Alberni during
the Depression in 1934 and the hospital at Esperanza in 1937 were
products of his vision and concern for those on the coast who had
little social contacts or care.

The Stranger's Rest was open for only a few years, but it was
available at the time when men who were otherwise homeless
and friendless needed it the most. Once jobs began to open up
and the economy strengthened, there was no further need for it.
The hospital, with its resident physician and surgeon, Dr. Herman
McLean, was the first medical facility for the greater section of the
west coast of Vancouver Island. Not only was the building Percy's
concern, but, as has been previously mentioned, he also spent time
looking for the best site on which to locate it.

Dr. McLean brought his family to the hospital after it had been built in late 1937. Things had gone well. God had miraculously provided the money to buy the land, and qualified nurses were called by God to serve there. Over the years, the complement of nurses grew as the hospital prospered. Some worked for a few years and then left, but others always came to replace them.

But then, unexpectedly, as sometimes happens when God's work is going forward, a letter arrived from the Shantymen's head office. It informed Dr. McLean that their mission was dedicated to itinerant work and not established stationary missions. The import of the letter was that the Shantymen's association would not continue to support the hospital.

This was a severe blow not only to the McLean family, who had sold everything to move permanently to the hospital, but also to Percy, who had sponsored the doctor and brought him to the west coast. A solution to the dilemma had to be found quickly, or the hospital would have to close. Percy assured the McLean family that he would do all he could to help the hospital set up as a mission organization, but that they would have to trust God for their funding, even as he did.

A Board of Directors was formed on which Percy served, and the hospital was registered as a mission organization with the Canadian government. Dr. McLean, his family and the staff soon realized that God was faithful to provide not only the financial needs but the continuing staff needs as well. God is ever faithful to His promises. We just need to believe His Word and act on it.

The *Willis Shank*

In 1948, Percy met a couple in Seattle who dreamed of using a post-war naval vessel as a floating hospital. The husband was in the construction business but felt God calling him into missionary service. As their friendship grew, "Cap" Stabbert told Percy of his desire. He purchased a naval minesweeper from the United States government and began to refit it as a hospital ship. He incorporated the mission under the name Marine Medical Mission (now North American Indigenous Ministries). Plans went ahead, and the ship was soon set to make its maiden voyage in July 1949, with Percy on board.

The ship was dedicated in Victoria during the same ceremony as the *Messenger III* and the *Bruce McLean.* Captain C. F. Stabbert christened the boat the *Willis Shank,* named for a young Seattle Youth for Christ leader who was killed in an airplane crash on his way to Alaska to dedicate a new mission. Plans were made for the ship to visit the sparsely populated islets off the coast of British Columbia and Alaska and provide medical and spiritual help to the indigenous people at its ports of call.

According to their Website (www.NAIM.ca) when the *Willis Shank* arrived at a new port, the crew would blare Christian music from a bullhorn speaker up on the mast. When people heard the music, they would gather at the dock to welcome the ship. While the ship was docked, one team would attend to the medical cases, one would hold meetings to preach the gospel, and, in the summer, Bible college students would volunteer to hold Bible study classes.

Percy told me of one instance of God's miraculous provision for this ship as it approached Bella Coola, B.C., intending to hold some children's meetings there. As a ship of American registry, the captain had to request permission from the Canadian authorities to put in at that port. The permission was denied, and the ship had to continue northward to Alaska.

However, God must have had a purpose for them at Bella Coola, because the engine soon began to experience problems and make unusual noises. The ship turned around and again radioed for permission to pull into port in an emergency. This time permission was granted, and the ship tied up at the wharf.

The ship's engineer tried to discover the cause of the engine trouble. While he and his crew began dismantling the suspected parts, others in the crew with time on their hands decided to see if they could hold some Bible classes for the children. The repairs would take a few days until the ship was ready to sail again.

When the engine crew finally found the problem, they were absolutely astounded. A bolt had come loose and gone through the reduction gear. Although the gear was not damaged, the teeth of the gears had crimped the bolt. Everyone who heard of the trouble and saw the bolt had to acknowledge that God had worked a miracle to get the *Willis Shank* into that port. The crew also recognized that God had made a way for them to tell the children the old, old story of Jesus and His love.

In 1959, the mission began placing full-time missionaries in the native communities, and the boat ministry came to a close. Ministry efforts onshore focused on the interior of western Canada.

Coastal Missions

After Percy had to retire, the *Messenger III* continued its endeavors with Harold Peters as skipper. Earl Johnson stayed on with Harold, and others came on board for short durations. The camping program kept them busy all summer long transporting young people, counselors and provisions to the various campsites.

When Harold retired, Earl Johnson skippered the *Messenger III* from 1960 to 1968. In 1968, a decision was made to sell the vessel to a private party in Victoria, who loved the ship and would keep it well maintained. Even now, after all these years, the *Messenger III* is still in mint condition.

A picture on the Coastal Missions website shows Harold Peters presenting the memorial plaque from the *Messenger III* to Don Robertson, the new superintendent, to be attached to the camper truck named *Messenger IV*. New roads had been built that opened up several more areas to vehicle traffic and expanded the range of a land-based ministry. By then, the Shantymen's Christian Association no longer seemed committed to the use of mission boats.

Working with Don Robertson were other new men, including Joe Ottom, Ron McKee and Roy Getman. Roy Getman had experience in maritime mission work and wanted to make a survey of coastal needs beyond Vancouver Island. Using the vessel *Nipentuck*, he gathered information that, when coupled with other appraisals, revealed a continuing need.

In 1973, a training program for new workers was instituted at Camp Ross, located at Pachena Bay, near Bamfield. The program included Bible studies and various aspects of navigation and seamanship training, including handling dories in the surf. Six oarsmen rowed each dory, with one person steering and giving rowing commands. Later, some of those involved attended seamanship classes at Camosun College in Victoria.

By 1974, Camp Ross, now commonly referred to as "Pachena," hosted a number of programs. A clinic was built and dedicated to serve the needs of hikers coming off the famous West Coast Trail. With its three-acre lawn and first aid building, the camp was a welcome sight to hikers—especially those with blisters, cuts and abrasions—and gave them the opportunity to finally relax at the end of their grueling trek up the trail from Port Renfrew.

In the mid-1970s, outreach was expanded to the Queen Charlotte Islands and southeast Alaska. Among those participating were three young women: Joan McKee, Gloria Troll and Debbie Forney. Gloria and Debbie worked in the Queen Charlotte Islands, and Joan worked at Camp Ross with her husband, Ron. In time there were others, including Brian Burkholder, Anne Spencer, Chet McArthur, Teresa Quesnel, Tom Maxie and George Loewen.

At one point, Roy Getman conducted a survey that revealed a continuing need for mission boat visitation. So Roy and some of the trainees at Pachena Bay built a small vessel and called it

CV-1. Being trailerable, the *CV-1* made it possible for crews to reach people living in remote places on the inside and outside coasts. Later, the fishing vessel *Kolberg* was made available to be used during its off-season months for fishing. Then, in late 1979, those involved in the project formed a new mission entity separate from the Shantymen's organization and incorporated it under the name "Coastal Missions Society." Although they made no appeals for money, the donations began to come in. These unsolicited provisions from God's people showed that the new mission could operate on a faith basis. Now, nearly 30 years later, it is thrilling to note that God has supplied the society's every need, without the need for its members to ask for money.

The group purchased a former government vessel in 1980 and named it *Coastal Messenger*. After a time of preparation, the ship began a large circuit using alternating crews. Meanwhile, land teams visited areas near the Strait of Georgia, in Bamfield near Pachena Bay, and south to Coos Bay, Oregon.

In 1981, the group decided it needed a Zodiac inflatable boat for the *Coastal Messenger*. Percy was there at the time, and as they were all together, he prayed, "Lord, we know You have a Zodiac up Your sleeve somewhere." Shortly thereafter, the group received a monetary gift big enough to purchase a new Zodiac, a 20-horsepower outboard motor *and* a spare propeller for the *Coastal Messenger*.

There was always a need for top equipment in coastal missionary endeavors. So, in the early 1990s, Roy Getman began designing a new steel ship to replace the wooden *Coastal Messenger*. His plans were checked and approved by a naval architect in Vancouver. The wooden *Coastal Messenger* was returned to its original name at the time of its sale, and the name *Coastal Messenger* was retained for the new ship launched at Esquimalt in September 1998. It was commissioned into full-scale missionary service in Victoria in April 1999.

Since that time, there has been much growth and expansion in the ministry. In answer to Percy's prayer that God not send any "misfits," new workers who are skilled in marine work are now involved.[1]

CHAPTER FIFTEEN

A FATHER AND A GRANDFATHER

And you, fathers, do not provoke your children to wrath, but bring
them up in the training and admonition of the Lord.
(Ephesians 6:4)

PERCY AND MARGARETTE were very good parents. They were even better grandparents—they just expanded the parental role to a wider field of grandchildren, which eventually numbered nine boys and girls. As these grandchildren grew to adulthood and married, great-grandchildren came along to be blessed, coddled and enjoyed by Bumpa and Nana.

I wasn't aware of Percy's parenting abilities until Margarette and I moved to Victoria in 1940. Until then, he had been home for only a few days at a time every six weeks or so. But once he was established in the big house on Belmont Avenue, Percy was home every day with us. That was when I found out what it was like to have my father wake me up in the morning for school and have both of my parents there when I got home again.

Frank, being seven years older, had been able to go on the boat with Percy a few times while we lived in Vancouver. When we moved, Frank decided to stay there and get a job until he could enlist in the Air Force during World War II.

Percy had an inventive streak that my Aunt Millie told me about. When she and Frank were young, Percy made an early version of a skateboard for them. He used hockey pucks for wheels and attached them to a board on which one could ride down the street. When Percy thought of patenting his idea, he was told no one would use it. He was way ahead of his time with that toy.

Percy also loved puns and humorous ditties. One of the verses about puns that I recall goes like this:

Oh, I wish I had a puni-shed
In which to hide my punnish head
So that for every little pun-I-shed
I might not be punish-ed.

We were used to living in a large family in Vancouver, and that, too, was expanded when Percy and Margarette opened the home for service personnel. It was rare for there to be just the three of us for dinner. Our house was usually filled with men and women from different parts of Canada, the United Kingdom and even the United States.

Percy made it a regular habit to rise early and have his time with the Lord before starting his day. In the winter, he stoked up the furnace so the house got warm. Then every school day, he came in and woke me up, closed the bedroom window, and went back to the kitchen to get breakfast ready. He did this so Margarette could have all the rest she needed before she took on the chores of the day.

My parents noticed that I had some musical ability and made sure I had piano lessons from a gifted teacher. The two of us worked together for the next several years as I progressed through the levels of theory and performance.

Leaving Home

My socialization that had begun in our Vancouver family continued as I became a younger sister to all the men who had left their families to serve in the armed forces. Margarette and Percy became surrogate parents to them, as many were still in their late teens and newly taken from their homes. There was an almost constant turnover as the young people they learned to love were transferred across Canada or overseas, and new ones came to take their places in our home and hearts.

I grew up in that environment, graduated from high school, began college and started work. In July 1949, I married Bob Billester and moved to southern California. This was a very difficult time for Margarette. She thought that I was too young and inexperienced to marry and that we didn't know each other well enough. She was right, but we were in love. I think Percy realized that I was committed to this step, and he probably helped Margarette realize it, too.

After a while, she gave us her blessing and began planning our nuptials. She was an excellent seamstress and made many pretty dresses for me as a child. This time, she outdid herself and made my wedding dress and trousseau. Her heart was heavy in this work, for she knew that Bob and I would be living far away from them and that visits would not be easy.

Both Bob and I were students at the Bible Institute of Los Angeles (Biola) in downtown Los Angeles. I graduated in 1951 and Bob in 1952. While still in college, Bob was asked to be a student pastor at a small church. He knew that God had called him to the ministry, and this was the first stop on that career that lasted until his death in 1975.

Bob and I had three boys: Stephen, Dale and John. When John was old enough to travel, we loaded up our car every August and drove to Victoria to spend vacations with Margarette and Percy.

Frank married Eileen Mahood while he was a senior at the University of British Columbia, the year after Bob and I married. He graduated first in his class with a Bachelor of Science degree in Pharmacy. He was a pharmacist for several years in Victoria, and then changed to a career in real estate. He and Eileen had three girls and three boys: Colleen (Luke), Murray, Glenn, Maura (Walls), Donna (Worth) and Dean. The first three were the same ages as our three boys, so all the cousins eagerly looked forward to their summer visits.

Family Visits

Percy and Margarette became "Bumpa" and "Nana" to all the grandchildren. I think the two of them looked forward to those visits as eagerly as my family did. They stocked up on juices, extra fruit and cookies in preparation for the arrival. They also patronized the fish and chip shop next door several times.

Looking back on those times, I have to wonder at the sudden impact my family of five had on the quiet life of the two grandparents. No sooner had the men unloaded the car and taken the suitcases to the bedrooms than the boys would run over to the grocery story for dried peas and peashooters. Then they would run up to their bedroom upstairs and practice shooting peas out of the window. (Dear Percy spent quite some time picking new pea plants out of his flowerbeds.)

The boys would then get on the telephone with their cousins, arranging outings and sleepovers. Percy took us all to a favorite beach to swim or a park to play on the equipment. Margarette was working part time each day and was not able to enjoy all of the fun. Bob couldn't wait to plan fishing trips with anyone who would join him.

Bob and I and Frank and Eileen got together to catch up on our lives. I took the opportunity to visit longtime friends. And, of course, we made sure to visit all the aunts and uncles, too.

My mother and I had our shopping days on the weekends. Margarette would tell Percy that we were going downtown, and he would offer to drive us there. "No," Margarette would say, "We'll take the bus." But Percy insisted on driving us to town and, once in the car, he would ask, "When should I pick you up? Do you think 45 minutes is enough?" Margarette would then tell him that this would not be enough time for us to find the items she was looking for, and so we would take the bus home. It was always such a special treat for me to go shopping with my mother. I enjoyed just being together and looking for exactly the right things we had in mind.

The highlight of our summer vacation was the family dinner at the Princess Mary restaurant. Percy reserved the big center table for about 15 or 16 people. It was quite a treat for our boys to experience this formal dining room and order what they wanted from the big menu. Percy would sit at the head of the table and look at Margarette, and then look at each grandchild with such pleasure. He would say, "Just look at these children! Nine of them, and each one is healthy and smart!" Then he would comment on how blessed we all were.

At the end of the meal, he would pull a fresh 50-dollar bill from his wallet and allow one or two of the older boys to take the money to pay the check. It made them feel so important and was such a thoughtful gesture on Percy's part.

Fond Memories

My nieces and nephews tell of times when Percy brought over a pot of soup and some of their favorite "sticky buns" from a local bakery. Percy and Margarette kept the communication lines open with all their children and grandchildren, and having meals together was one way to do that. Both were good cooks and prepared healthy meals for themselves and guests.

Percy loved fresh oysters and got some whenever he could. I remember watching him with awed fascination one day as he downed several raw ones that he had seasoned with a little vinegar, salt and pepper. His facial expression was one of sheer pleasure.

One granddaughter, Maura, remembered Percy meeting her at the front door by saying "Hello, my sweets!" The family sat around the table loaded with good food at the home on Cloverdale Avenue. After the meal was over, Percy asked one of them to read from a little book called *The Daily Light*. It contained a short collection of Scripture verses for each day. Then the meal was ended with a short prayer.

Maura remembered when Nana and Bumpa invited her and a girlfriend to stay overnight. As an additional treat, Percy took them bowling. He always seemed to be prepared with some fun thing for the children to do.

My oldest niece, Colleen, when young, asked Percy to make her a pair of stilts. It was an unusual request, but Percy did make a pair for her. She managed to get on them and walk around. When the cousins came up that summer, all the boys had a wonderful time seeing who could maneuver on them the longest.

Percy and Margarette's house on Cloverdale Avenue contained several interesting things that our sons didn't see often in California. One was a fairly large green glass ball that sat by the fireplace in the living room. It was a glass float used in a Japanese fishing net that had broken free and floated across the Pacific to where Percy could obtain it. In the back yard, there was a beautiful weeping willow tree. Its circle of branches drooped to the ground, providing a lovely shady area to sit and read in the summer. Percy loved his flowerbeds and hanging baskets, which made bright accents to the exterior of the home.

When I asked my son Stephen his memories of Bumpa, he told of Percy taking him to camp to perform his magic tricks. A more serious time was when he helped Bumpa clear out the apartment of another Shantymen missionary, Jack Spratt. Jack was the one who mailed the Shantymen's monthly paper and other Christian literature to a mailing list that reached around the globe. Jack had passed away, and all the literature and mailing lists had to be boxed up and stored.

When the day arrived for our family to pack up and begin the long trip home after a visit with Percy and Margarette, they would sometimes drive with us as far as Portland. We had a favorite motel there where we liked to stay because it had a swimming pool. There was also a go-cart track nearby, and you could rent one and drive around the track. The boys loved this place. One year, Margarette decided she would try it, even though she didn't know how to drive a car. We cheered her on for taking that kind of risk. Somewhere among our pictures is one of Nana helmeted, her skirt tucked around her legs, careering around the track. We all had a new respect for her after that.

On two or three occasions, Margarette and Percy drove all the way to California to visit our family. That was always a special time, and we loved to take them around to the various tourist attractions. Percy preached at Bob's church so the congregation could hear some of the wonderful things God had done on the mission field. The church always looked forward to their coming and were really blessed by the things Percy taught them about God's faithfulness and provision.

CHAPTER SIXTEEN

RETIREMENT

*Even to your old age, I am He, and even to gray
hairs I will carry you! I have made and I will
bear; Even I will carry and will deliver you.*
(Isaiah 46:4)

TOWARD THE END of his time on the *Messenger III*, Percy
experienced a number of serious events that affected his
health and forced him to leave the maritime work. One of
these incidents was as follows:

In 1949 I had the misfortune to fall overboard on a miserable,
foggy night in the Pacific. The air was cold and damp and the
water was frigid. By the grace of God I was preserved. As there
was no heat on board, I shivered throughout the night with no
change of clothes to relieve the distress. I was delivering a new
boat to one of our bases on the coast.

For some months I had known that some evil thing was
working inside my body, and the symptoms were becoming more
acute. This wetting [from the fall off the boat] merely hastened
the effects. As soon as we had delivered the new craft, I caught a

plane over the mountains to join another of our boats as she was heading north to Alaska. I had hardly joined the second boat, before I knew that I would be forced to seek medical aid. My wife and I excused ourselves from the trip and caught a southbound ship for home. By the time I arrived, I was a stretcher case.

My wife and I were feeling rather bad when the doctors told me that my days on the field were at an end and that, like Jacob, I should be dragging my right leg around for the rest of my life. While they told me this they were solemn faced, indeed. But when I replied that they could give me a dozen "gammy" legs, if they would give me the "power with God" that Jacob received, they relaxed and grinned.

It was a dark day for both of us. In our youth we had given our strength to the Lord and were happy in the giving. We had known poverty, hunger, weakness, and pain in carload lots, but it had always been a source of joy to know that we were suffering these things for His Name's sake. My wife had gone to work in an office to help keep the Lord's work going, giving largely of her strength and energy, as well as her resources. Sometimes she said, "You go back to the field and keep the Lord's work going, and He will take care of us here." Often there was no income, little food for our children, and second-hand clothes for us all, but they were days happy beyond measure.

Now to be cut down, useless, and with no further resources to squander on our blessed Savior, we felt really impoverished. But, do you know, since that day Jesus Christ has commenced to pour His blessings upon us in a greater way than we could have dreamed—in basket, and in store, as well as in heart and soul! Strangely enough, our hours of service for Him are longer, and His presence is more "visible" than ever before.

A missionary has a right to expect God to keep him actively useful until he dies even though he be bedridden or use a wheel chair.

(PW)

When Percy was hospitalized, Margarette phoned my husband and me in California to inform us of his condition. I could not be with my parents at that time, but I assured them that we would have our church pray for them as well. The Shantymen's luncheon group joined with us and all the other friends to pray for Percy's recovery and return to health. God was merciful, and Percy was restored to us for many more years of example in faith and service and his deep love for the Lord.

Earl Johnson told me of an accident Percy had on board the *Princess Maquinna*. The ship was heaving and rolling in a violent sea off Cape Beale, and Percy lost his balance and fell against a metal piece, damaging his shoulder and back. The injury resulted in years of back pain and progressive hand tremors, and it may also have caused a frozen shoulder, as he had trouble raising his arm for a long time following this accident.

I recently talked with Tim Bird, who has ministered for 20 years to the unchurched people in Port McNeill at the north end of Vancouver Island. He described his first meeting with Percy Wills. He had heard quite a bit about Percy and was looking forward to meeting him. Tim expected him to be a young man, but he didn't have any description to go by. He attended a service and chanced to sit next to an older man he did not know. During the meeting as they were worshiping the Lord, Tim heard a loud "snap." Looking at the man next to him, he saw him raise his arm and say, "Praise the Lord! I can raise my hand right up, and I haven't been able to do that for years!" He later learned that the man sitting beside him was Percy Wills. He didn't look anything like Tim expected. Percy was an older man, but he was young in spirit.

Percy's back continued to give him problems. During family vacations in Victoria, I often saw him supporting himself with his arms as he leaned over the sink and peeled potatoes for supper. He did not give in to the pain, but it was evident on his face. Yet all the while as he was preparing the vegetables, he would frequently say quietly and with feeling, "Praise the Lord."

One summer several years later, I noticed that he was walking normally with a spring in his step. I asked him how he had got rid of the pain, and he told me that it had happened while he was crawling around the grass and picking out the weeds. It seemed quite unconventional, and I am sure that the Lord was working to heal him. However, his hand tremors continued to increase in intensity.

Continuing to Serve

Although these tremors hampered Percy, he did not stop serving the Lord. He just moved to other activities. Someone said of him that as his physical range diminished, his spiritual vision grew and spread outward. Some of those visions later became realities.

On one of our vacation trips, I learned of another aspect of Percy's service mentality. An older Christian man had a blood disorder that required frequent transfusions. Percy found that he had the same blood type and became the donor for this gentleman as often as possible. His selflessness gave this man a few more years of life with his wife and family.

The year 1970 was the fortieth anniversary of Percy's missionary status with the Shantymen's Christian Association. To honor him on this occasion, a celebration was planned. Someone had the idea to send a notice out to a large mailing list of friends, relatives and others who knew of his work. In the notice was a request that the recipients write letters to Percy relating some memorable instance that meant much to them or congratulations for his many years of quiet service to the Lord. Dozens of people from the west coast of Vancouver Island, across Canada and even into the United States sent letters as they were directed.

Once all the letters had been received, they were gathered in a book with a hardbound cover and titled *Tributes to a Shantyman Percy E. Wills*. The gathering was an evening of joy and reminiscence for all who attended, especially for Percy and Margarette. It was a wonderful thing to watch Margarette and Percy read through each of the letters that reminded them of the dear friends they had made through the years. That book is now in my possession, and it is still a thing of joy to read those letters, even though I don't recognize many of the names.

Margarette was still working at the credit union at the time. One day, she discovered that if she could organize a tour group of government employees to go to Hawaii, she and Percy could both go at no cost. She got busy and signed up the required number for the week's tour. Everyone had a wonderful time, and they all decided to do the same thing the following year.

Last Christmas with Margarette

At the end of 1969, my family was invited to spend Christmas in Victoria. My husband, Bob Billester, pastored a church, and Christmas season was an extremely busy time for us. I worked full-time as well. But since we had never been able to spend Christmas with my parents, we decided we would do it.

Our two youngest sons were in high school, and the oldest was a freshman in college. He thought he should stay home and get a job to help pay his tuition costs. We told him that this could be our last trip as a family to Margarette and Percy's and that we wanted him to go. I had managed to save up some vacation time for the trip. My husband made arrangements for visiting ministers to lead the services at the church in our absence. We finished the rest of the planning and got ready to leave.

Because snow had been forecast for the area, we decided to leave late in the evening so that we could cross the mountain range between Los Angeles and Bakersfield before the storm came. Bob's grandmother thought that we should stay home, get a good night's sleep and leave very early the next morning. "No," Bob said, "I think we need to leave tonight." His grandmother was quite concerned that we would be traveling while tired, but he felt strongly that we should go as planned. It was providential that we did not wait.

We left and drove through the night, successfully crossing the Ridge Route, as it is known. Early the next morning when we listened to the news on the radio, we learned that because of heavy snow, the Ridge Route had closed at midnight. God had been with us so that we were not delayed on our way.

We had made this trip to vacation with my parents every August, so it was most unusual for us to see the familiar scenery now covered with snow. It was beautiful in a different way, and we enjoyed it. When we got to Seattle the next evening, it started to snow and driving became difficult. In the dark, the headlights showed the snow coming straight at the windshield. It was mesmerizing, so we pulled into the nearest motel for the night. The boys had never seen snow falling and were entranced by it. They all stood outside with their mouths open and tongues out to catch the snowflakes.

We phoned ahead to let the family know of our delay, and then got back on the road in the morning. We crossed the border into Canada and headed for the ferry that would take us across the straits to Victoria. The boys' excitement grew onboard, for they knew that Nana and Bumpa's house was only a couple of hours away.

We spent a wonderful Christmas with my parents, and they enjoyed seeing the boys, who were reaching adulthood. While we were there, Margarette said that she was arranging another tour to Hawaii in April and wanted the family to join them. We declined, because we did not think we could vacation again so soon, even though it would have been a wonderful opportunity. We returned home, not knowing that our boys would never see Nana alive again.

Their memories would always be good ones of seeing her healthy and enjoying life.

It was unforeseen, but the tour to Hawaii was devastating to Margarette. As it happened, one woman who was ill with the flu joined the tour. Margarette caught it just as the tour was ending. Then, when Percy and Margarette arrived in Victoria, word awaited them that Margarette's mother had passed away the day before. Without unpacking, the two flew back to Vancouver to attend her funeral. The combination of grief, illness and weariness compromised Margarette's immune system, and she became ill. Percy took her to the emergency room, where she was diagnosed with double pneumonia. She spent some time in the hospital to clear her lungs and have her heart carefully monitored.

When Margarette was finally released to go home, the doctor put her on a strict diet and told her that she needed to rest. Her heart was so weakened by the disease that she would never be able to return to her former activities.

As soon as Percy saw how serious Margarette's situation was, he resigned from the Shantymen's Christian Association and every other Christian group with which he was involved. He devoted himself to her complete care and made sure she had everything she needed. If there were anything that might improve her strength and prolong her life, he did it.

I phoned frequently to see how my mother was doing. Sometimes I was able to talk with her, but if not, then Percy gave me the current information. Because I was working full time, I could not be with Margarette to help care for her. My brother was also in ill health and needed care, and Margarette's sister, who lived in Ontario Province in Canada, also could not be with her.

This state of affairs lasted for several months, with Margarette getting no better. In fact, she began to weaken. One day, Percy phoned me to say that I should come up to see my mother. She had been re-admitted to the hospital, but doctors said there was nothing they could do for her.

Saying Goodbye

When I got to Victoria, Percy immediately took me to the hospital to visit Margarette. I was shocked to see how thin my mother had become. Her features had sharpened, and she was just lying still. I spent a few days visiting her and then returned home.

Ten days later, Percy phoned me to tell me that Margarette had passed away. The year was 1972. Once more I flew to Victoria, but this time it was for the funeral.

The chapel was packed with people who loved Margarette and had been blessed by her life. Percy was composed and quiet in his mourning. When he spoke, his face was radiant with the peace of God. His voice was strong as he told of God's presence with them during the months when there was just the two of them. The service was comforting, because everyone knew she was with the Lord. We thanked God that she was out of weakness and pain.

Margarette's memorial service was held that Sunday at the Central Baptist Church. It, too, was full of people who wanted to honor her life. Many spoke of what she had meant to them. Some were former servicemen who had been at their home at 2024 Belmont Avenue during the war. It was interesting to me that several who spoke mentioned Margarette's gracious hospitality and her cooking.

Everyone who knew her loved Margarette. Her life was full, and she had accomplished much more with a heart problem than many others had who were in good health. She was a mentor to many young women and had even started a fellowship group for Christian nurses. She enjoyed the board meetings for the Shantymen's committee that met in their home and always provided tasty refreshments with the tea.

After I returned home, I phoned Percy frequently. I was struck by the flat tone of his voice. Formerly, there was always a lilt when he answered my calls, but now it was as if he were responding to a stranger. He was always the strong one in the family, and we all relied on him. He kept close to the Lord and took God's Word as his direction. In his grief, I believe he continued that practice. The Lord was his comfort and confidant, and I don't know that he went to anyone else for help or counsel. But he had many godly friends who came to visit and pray with him.

Margarette's death was not the only occasion of sadness. Within the next year or so their son, Frank, became quite ill and needed the care of a specialist. Percy found a doctor in Vancouver who was able to diagnose his problem, and he accompanied Frank to his appointments. When Frank was hospitalized, Percy attended to his affairs. Frank also suffered several heart attacks, which weakened him and severely affected his business.

In 1973, my husband was diagnosed with cancer and began treatment in California. Percy gave me great comfort when I called him with the news, encouraging us to trust God for the grace to endure whatever He allowed. He reminded me that God healed either by grace or by glory. As it turned out, God healed my husband, Bob, by grace through the gate of death in 1975.

Percy did not rejoin the Shantymen's Association after Margarette's death. Changes in personnel and practice at the head office in Toronto caused a difference in vision for the work on Vancouver Island. There had been little on-site supervision by their board members over the years, so some of their newer directives were not applicable to the west-coast work. One directive was that the missionaries were to work singly, not as teams, though the single women had to work together for safety. The SCA also decided that the missionaries didn't need big boats but could use planes instead. This was not a practical method of ministry on the west coast. These decisions were a cause of sadness to Percy.

A fellow missionary, who was at one of the meetings in Victoria, told me that the president of the association had even treated Percy most disrespectfully. I was angered when I heard this, even though the incident had taken place several years ago. I don't think the president knew the effectiveness of the work that Percy and the other missionaries had done. He was not aware of the great sacrifices these men and their wives had made for the work. True to his character, Percy never mentioned such treatment to anyone. He simply trusted the Lord to work the situation out. Rather than complaining, he began putting his efforts into helping other young groups get started in the mission field.

CHAPTER SEVENTEEN

A NEW LIFE

Every good gift and every perfect gift is from above, and comes
down from the Father of lights . . .
(James 1:17)

ONE DAY IN early 1974, Frank phoned me and said, "Sis! You'll never guess what just happened!" His voice was charged with excitement.

"What happened, Frank?" I asked curiously.

Again, he said, "Sis! You'll never guess what just happened!"

I repeated the question. The third time he repeated his remark, I said, "Frank! Tell me what happened!"

"Dad's getting married!" he said.

My jaw dropped. I was thunderstruck! Thoughts began whizzing around in my head. *Who was this woman who had gotten her hooks into my dad? Was she good enough for him? Where did he meet her?* I had never known that he was interested in another woman or even considered the fact that he might remarry. Had I thought about it, I would have realized that Percy's loving nature had to have someone with whom to share that love.

Percy had told me that he was going to Toronto to be interviewed by Douglas C. Percy for the book he was writing about the history of the Shantymen's work. I never dreamed Percy had another reason for the trip. That reason turned out to be Vera Coulter McPherson, one of the four Coulter girls whom Percy and Margarette knew from their early days in the ministry. They had maintained contact through all the years and visited together whenever the occasion arose. She, too, had lost her spouse. At that time, she was the dean of women at a Bible college in Ontario Province.

Here is the story from Percy's letter to me of January 21, 1974, in which he told me of his engagement:

A year ago, Vera came out to visit one of her daughters who is living here in the city, and when she phoned me I asked her out for lunch at the Princess Mary. She was her usual delightful self—half Irish, half Angel. I must say I was decidedly smitten, but I did not breathe a word to her or anyone else, for I could not see how any woman, let alone Vera could take a second look at a broken down old backwoodsman. But I did hear from her a couple of times, and something she wrote made me feel that perhaps she was interested in continuing our friendship on a more intimate plane. As I was going east on business anyway, I wrote informing her I would be in Toronto, and if she were free for the weekend I would be most happy to take her out for dinner.

To my amazement I found that she felt quite taken with your old dad and after we had had a couple of meals together and spent a good deal of time in her apartment at the college chatting, I asked her a sixty-four dollar question, and told her to think it over, and if. . . . Before I left on the Sunday evening, she gave me a definite reply in the affirmative. I had taken a couple of rings along, just in case . . .

You can imagine the wagging of the tongues of all the college kids when they saw your old dad going in and out of a widow's apartment and then accompanying her to church on Sunday morning. So we decided to make the announcement immediately to the heads of the college.

(PW)

As it turned out, not only was Vera "good enough" for Percy, but she was also a perfect partner for him. Not every woman would have fit his lifestyle. Percy was well known and had a wide circle of friends, acquaintances and interests. He was hospitable. If he saw someone at church who seemed to be a stranger in town, he invited the person home for lunch. When friends from out of town visited, he insisted that they stay at his home. He picked up their luggage before they had a chance to bend over and deposited it in the guest room. I was told that he had a practice of asking the husband's shoes to be put outside the bedroom door. Percy would shine and replace them before the guests were up in the morning.

Vera had the same gift of hospitality. Her husband had spent many years as a pastor, so she was used to entertaining, having company from out of town, and sharing her husband's time with his parishioners. Also, her long-term friendship with Percy and Margarette gave her great insights about him.

Their wedding was held in Toronto at the home of Vera's daughter. Frank and Eileen flew in from Victoria to attend. Millie and Milton, Percy's sister- and brother-in-law, drove down from their home north of Toronto to join them. They were all happy to surround Percy and Vera with love and congratulations at this joyous start of a new life.

My husband, Bob, was undergoing cancer treatments at the time, but I was able to be away from him for a few days and attend the ceremony. However, my trip was not without difficulty. The night before I was scheduled to leave, I had a phone call from a friend near Toronto who told me that there was a strike at the Toronto airport and that I should call the airline to check if my morning flight had been cancelled. It had not, but neither was I flying directly into Toronto. The flight had been redirected to land at Ottawa and, after a four-hour wait, I would have a seat on a flight to Toronto.

The arrangements that Percy had made for meeting me at the airport now had to be changed, but I had no way to get hold of him. I called my friend back to tell her of the changes, and she arranged for one of the Shantymen's committee to meet me and take me to the hotel where Percy and Vera had reserved a room for me. When I finally arrived at the Toronto airport, I tried to think how I could word an announcement to let the person meeting me know that I was there, but not let others know that I was traveling alone. Finally, the man who was to meet me approached and introduced himself. He took my luggage and said he was parked quite close to the entrance. However, when we got outside, his car was not there.

He had, in fact, parked close to the entrance, but in his haste to meet me he had parked in a rental car spot, and his car had been towed away. He was an executive in a large corporation, and when he called about his car, it was returned immediately. He drove me to the hotel and accompanied me to the registration desk. I was grateful for all he had gone through to meet me, and I thanked him for his trouble.

Finally, at about 11:30 P.M., Percy and Vera arrived. They had been to the graduation ceremony at the college where Vera was dean of women. Had the strike not taken place, they would have met me in the afternoon, and I would have been able to attend the ceremony with them.

God had indeed brought Percy and Vera together. It was wonderful once again to hear the lilt in his voice when I phoned him. Percy joined the church choir, and he and Vera volunteered twice a week to be phone counselors for the radio program *100 Huntley Street*, hosted by David Mainse. They suited each other so well and were happy together for the 16 years given them.

CHAPTER EIGHTEEN

FINISHING THE RACE

I have fought the good fight, I have fin-
ished the race, I have kept the faith.
(2 Timothy 4:7)

P ERCY AND VERA moved into a senior apartment complex
next door to the church they attended. Their fixed income
was small, but adequate for their needs. Percy had never
worried about money. If he had some ready cash and knew another
person needed it, he gave his money away. My father-in-law, Michael
Billester, once sent Percy a donation and was quite upset when he
learned that Percy had given it to someone else. When he asked
Percy why he hadn't used it for himself, Percy replied that he didn't
need it at the time. That was Percy's lifelong practice, for he knew
that God would always supply his need.

Percy and Vera were among friends they had known for a long
time in this apartment building. They were quite happy with the
move and enjoyed the visits and fellowship in that place. But then
Vera began to have memory problems, or "senior moments," as
they are often called. Her daughter and family lived in town, and

they often visited. My brother, Frank, and his second wife, Sheila, kept in close contact and often brought dinner to them. They, too, became aware of Vera's failing memory.

In their small apartment, it was easy for Percy to watch Vera to be sure she didn't leave a pot of soup on to boil dry or turn the oven on and forget what she had put in there. Despite this problem, she remained her cheery, loving self.

In the summer, they occasionally went to the church campground in Coburg, Ontario, where they could spend a week or two among Vera's friends and family. This was the plan for the summer of 1990. However, when Vera became quite anxious about the trip, it was called off.

In July, Percy realized he had something physically wrong with him. He made an appointment with his doctor to find out the cause. The diagnosis indicated that surgery was necessary, and the date was set. Percy called me to let me know of the situation, and I flew up to be with Vera during his hospitalization. I had just retired and was free to spend the time with them. Vera's memory loss had progressed to the point that she could not be left alone. I stayed with her during the day, and Vera's granddaughter spent the night in the apartment.

The surgery was successful, and Percy began to recuperate. Donnel McLean, who loved Percy like a father, was among his visitors. I still remember seeing the two of them walking down the hallway arm in arm, talking together. Their deep regard for each other was very apparent. Percy had often revealed things to Donnel that he had shared with no one else.

When Percy was able to return home, I flew back to California. I kept in contact with him and with my brother. He and Sheila brought dinner to them two or three nights a week to help them out. Other friends in the apartment complex also checked in on them. Percy still needed to watch over Vera to keep their life calm and quiet so that no sudden changes in their routine would cause her anxiety.

Waking up in Heaven

This state of affairs lasted until October. Percy was still recuperating from his surgery, and one afternoon he said that he was tired and wanted to take a nap. He lay down on the couch to sleep and woke up in heaven. The date was October 12, 1990.

Both families were notified of Percy's death. Vera's older daughter and a son flew immediately to Victoria to be with her. Frank, Sheila and I met with Vera's son and daughter and went with them to make the funeral arrangements. They had to pack up the apartment and take Vera with them when the funeral was over. They wondered if Vera's loss of memory might possibly spare her grief over Percy's death.

Many friends came for the funeral, several of whom were from out of town. One friend representing the SCA flew in from Toronto to be there. When I said to him, "You flew all the way out for the funeral?" he responded in full explanation by saying, "He was my friend."

While it was a solemn occasion, it was not really sad. Reverend Robert Holmes and Reverend Michalski conducted the service. One of the Scripture verses quoted was, "We thank God for every remembrance of him" (Phil. 1:3). The pastor commented that Percy taught by example and that, in his senior status, his spiritual vision had grown in range and continued to spread while his physical range had diminished. Then he repeated a quote from *Splendour From the Sea*, when Percy listed the three things we must believe: (1) God is in all things, (2) God can do the incredible, and (3) God can do the impossible.

The Scripture reading was 2 Timothy 4:7, where Paul writes, "I have fought the good fight, I have finished the race, I have kept the faith." That verse was Percy's life summed up in one sentence. Frank and I wrote the eulogy that Reverend Holmes read. Several people spoke of Percy's character, his influence in their lives, the great scope of his ministry and his implicit faith in God's providence, among other things. The heartfelt comments of all who spoke gave a broad picture of Percy's personality and influence.

Rick McPherson, Vera's son, spoke of the three ingredients a father needs to pass on: time, affection and attention. He said, "Percy was a wonderful father and grandfather. He was practical, loving, gracious, generous and a doer of the Word." Then he quoted a poem that may have been written by Percy:

To be with Christ, indeed would be the ultimate in ecstasy,
To roam the farthest realms of space,
To scale the topmost tors* of matchless grace,
To race with angels in their speed
Performing all their golden deeds.
Returning every now and then
To praise the Lord with cherubim.
To sit with Christ upon His throne
And nevermore to be alone.
No cold nor heat, no pain nor tears,
No counting time by days or years,
No tendency to live in sin,
No ugly hate without, within.

*Rocky outcroppings formed by weathering, particularly in England

Frank's two oldest children, Colleen Luke and Murray Wills, each gave tribute to Bumpa. Colleen mentioned Nana looking for "Per" while supper was cooking and noting the kitchen was the hub of activity in the home. She recalled the mission barrels in the basement filled with donated clothing that the cousins often used to dress up in.

Colleen's memory of Bumpa was of him fixing the tire swing and getting the beanbag toss ready for playtime. She spoke of seeing him on his knees in prayer early in the morning. She emphasized that he *knew* Jesus. He had the ability to love beyond others in a way that undergirded them and incorporated them. He wanted to really know how they were doing. He had specific questions about each person and what his or her interests were. He always seemed to know when one of them needed him. Then she told about a man who had once spoken with her father, Frank, about Percy. The man said that he was not a churchgoing person, but that Percy Wills was the closest to a saint as any person he had ever known. That was high praise, but Percy would have diminished the accolade to him, remarking that we are all saints.

When it was Murray's turn, he told of all that his Bumpa had meant to him. "He was a great man and very special to me and to all of us," he said. He told of how Percy had meant different things to different people, how he was always ready to embrace anyone in need, and how he was positive and had an open mind and the ability to love. Then Murray quoted several phrases of Percy's that were memorable to him, such as, "How wonderful!" and "You're so precious." He noted how Percy pronounced the word "*exquisite*," with the emphasis on the first syllable. Murray closed his talk by thanking Vera for the 16 years of their life together and for her love and care for Percy.

Following the grandchildren, the pastor read Psalm 107, particularly verses 23-32 that speak of those who go down to the sea in ships. It was one of Percy's favorite passages of Scripture, for the great meaning it had for him. Then the pastor made this statement: "The names of Johnson, Wills, Peters and McLean will shine in glory like gold on black velvet." (All of the families named were so loved, particularly on Vancouver Island.)

Earl Johnson, the "young missionary" in *Splendour From the Sea,* began by thanking our family for "sharing Percy with so many of us." He called Percy a universal man, a tremendous mentor, a man of the Spirit and a "helper of your joy" (2 Cor. 1:24). He told how Percy would turn around a negative comment to talk about faith, hope, prayer and the love we had. Earl listed three qualities of Percy's life: (1) his faith that trusted God for everything, (2) the Spirit in which he moved—he walked with, listened for and obeyed God—and (3) the quality of Percy's ministry, in which nothing was too small to tackle.

Reverend Holmes concluded the service with a few remarks, saying that Percy was a living epistle of God's grace. He said that all the graces of Galatians 5 were evident in his life, and they were. Percy did a good work, poured out his life in his ministry and has received the reward of God. Each one of those statements is true of Percy's life.

Percy was cremated, and his ashes were placed in Margarette's grave in Victoria. But, as he once said, "Christians never say 'goodbye' for the last time."

PERCY WILLS' STATEMENT OF FAITH

I HAVE ALWAYS contended, and still maintain, that the life of faith in Christ Jesus is the most adventurous life there is. Then, too, the man who believes God does not become a beggar, nor does he depend on man, Christian or non-Christian, to provide his needs. Nor is the life of faith a way whereby the Lord puts a man through trials and difficulties just to see how much he can stand. Rather, it is to prove to man His wonderful power and the potentiality that lies in the way of a man to exploit, if he only will. In other words, to prove to man His faithfulness, God has promised to do many things for some people, and some things for all people, but to the believer He lavishly pours out the cream of His storehouse. "Much more to them that believe."

It is quite possible for a person to have a natural faith, that is, to put his trust in man, or things, or earthly force, and accomplish a certain amount. But it takes faith in God Almighty to pull down strongholds and restore the dead to life. It is an entirely different matter to believe on the Lord Jesus Christ. The faith of the Son of God is that which makes all things possible.

Now, many people wish to see things accomplished, but they have no faith. It results in, "Show me the result, and I'll believe." They do not understand that such a thing is an impossibility in any walk of life, as well as the spiritual. When a man goes out on a business venture, he first believes that it is possible to succeed, or he would not commence. Even crooks hope to get away with their crookedness, or they would not crack their first safe. But in spiritual matters, men say, "Show me and I'll believe."

[Benjamin] Franklin believed that there was power in the lightning, and he went out with a kite and a key. He got results *after* he believed. Sir Robert Simpson believed there was such a thing as anesthetic, and he explored and found it. This is true of all knowledge: first faith, and then the fact. But things of time and sense are limited to their own time and sphere; faith in God is universal and unlimited. It may be employed by the fool as well as the intelligent man; by woman as well as man; by the old as well as young. All classes and creeds may come, and believe, and receive. That is the order. In His name, men have subdued kingdoms, wrought righteousness, and turned the violence of the sword. They are still doing it. Praise God!

In the field of natural forces, a man must be highly skilled in a limited and specialized manner to turn his theories into facts. In Christ Jesus, it is oftentimes the little child, the laboring man, or the charwoman who hits the target long before the intelligent man has come to his senses. The child will believe God in any circumstance, or any field, and get results.

In the world, a man may wonder whether he is acceptable for some particular field of endeavor. With Christ, any man may come and receive liberally, without being upbraided for his lack of knowledge.

Now faith is a peculiar thing. It is not acquired by study. A man may study about it, may watch it in operation for years, but until he puts the power to use himself, he gets nowhere. It is a gift of God, as much as love, and peace, and hope—"the gift of faith."

Faith is far greater than a mere mental assent to some given statement of creed. It is an operation, an experimentation. When a man says, "I believe," it does not necessarily mean that he *does* believe. He must utilize it, or demonstrate it. The difference between an active and a passive faith is the same as currycombing a dead mule, and a live one, when you get around his hocks. The dead one stays where he is, but the live one will react in a manner which is not easily foreseen, but *it does react*. A passive faith says much but does nothing. A live faith has no time to talk, for it is too busy.

When faith is employed in God, it is a progressive thing. It cannot stand still. The believer finds himself drawn out far beyond what he has seen before. New horizons continually beckon to further fields and greater heights, "from faith unto faith." There is no settling on the lees, no time for sitting on the hunkers. There is only progress or stagnation with the Lord. Many a chap has started his race well, only to become content with dogmas and creeds, and then wondered where the vital living breath had gone from his inner soul. He became wrapped up in business and other things, where he often succeeded, but leanness had come to his soul.

Here is a matter which has always entertained me, and which has caused me to wonder. "Add to your faith, experience, and to experience, hope, which maketh not ashamed" (Rom. 5:4-5; 2 Pet. 1:5 KJV). Every step the believer takes must be made by naked faith. The reason is easily seen. No exigencies are ever the same. Each legal problem, each financial tangle has new facets which need a new understanding. Each spiritual temptation comes with a new potentiality, which must be met by a new faith in the Bishop and Shepherd of our souls.

Now, each time a believer has been met by temptation or trial, and the God of his faith has delivered him from his trouble, the matter has become an experience. So it goes—step of faith, then deliverance, then experience. After a while, there dawns in the heart of the believer a wonderful light—God has never failed him.

Ebenezer. "Hitherto hath the Lord helped us" (1 Sam. 7:12 KJV). This is confidence, or hope, which is never ashamed in any kind of problem, for it knows that the Lord has never failed in the past. We have a strong hope that He is with us *now*. Ebenezer becomes Emmanuel, "God with us." Therefore, we may boldly say, "The Lord is my helper. I will not fear. What can man do unto me?" (Heb. 13:6). That sort of hope is never ashamed in the face of man or devil. A man may be surrounded by many and great enemies, in many environments, but he finds that the God of all grace is greater than them all. In physical, material, or spiritual things, the believer is matured, and his faith causes him to walk with strong confidence, quiet and serene.

The man of faith does not walk by experience. He does not say, "I have been tempted financially before, so I know what to do here." He simply approaches his heavenly Father and says, "Here is the old sinner whom you have invited to come. I am without strength, and I do not know how to approach this problem, but my eyes are on the Lord, and I expect you to save me, not because I deserve it, but because You said You would. Oh, Lamb of God, I come."

Experience does not teach you "how" to meet the new problem of the day. It merely teaches you the all-important fact that *God will not fail you in it.*

There seems to be another important characteristic of faith. At least, it always attends the work of true faith; that is, thanksgiving. The children of Israel moved out into the desert from Egypt, anxious and willing to leave the bonds and imprisonment, and to reach the Promised Land. But, as each new problem arose, they murmured and complained. In spite of all the miracles they had seen, they still rebelled.

For a person to say he cannot believe is a falsehood. God never asked a man to do an impossible thing. God does the impossible. He just asks us to believe that He can and will. Every man has the seed germ of faith within himself. All he needs to do is plant it. He can believe, if he will. Let him not say, "I cannot," but "I will not." Or better, "I will believe," in place of "I can."

As each new difficulty arose in the path of the Israelites, they disbelieved, but Moses believed God. His faith carried two million unbelieving people across the desert. What would have happened if they, too, had believed the Lord? One would think that after several such deliverances, the skeptics would have been cured. They had all been baptized (1 Cor. 10:2). They were all Israelites, but they were all destroyed except for the three who believed God. There was neither faith nor thanksgiving.

The order of their action was: first the problem, then the complaint, next the deliverance, and then the dance. Anyone can do that. In fact, almost everyone does. But it takes a healthy Christian to dance and praise the Lord in the midst of the fire and in the face of the foe. For him, there is a joy and peace known to no other person. Standing face to face with the enemy, he defies him to do his worst, while praising and blessing the God of his salvation, *while the issue is still in doubt.* Giving thanks to God and shouting Hallelujah in the face of the devil, just when he tells you that you are licked—that is adventure to satisfy the heart of any man. That is what the hearts of young folk crave after, when they say, "I want to *live my life.*"

The apostle Paul skimmed the cream of all his experience when he said, "I take pleasure *in* necessities, *in* persecutions, *in* distresses…" (2 Cor. 12:10 KJV). Now, those words were not included to fill up space. They were real and proven. Here is the greatest joy the Christian can know. Why did he not say that his pleasure came after deliverance? He said, "*in.*" He had learned to stand still as he entered into the trial, and there he praised the Lord and quietly waited for the God of his salvation. There came the peace that passes knowledge and understanding. Reversing the order of the Israelites, he sang the praises of God, and then was immediately delivered from the sting, if not the presence, of his test.

The employment of faith implies that there are two parties: one impotent, and one with force or power sufficient to meet the need. It also implies that the party of the second part not only is able, but willing to supply the want of the needy person. And lastly, that the party of the first part desires the aid of the able and willing individual.

Now, in all the little writings which we may publish and in all sermons which we may preach, there is one great desire. To make known, not the little accomplishments, which are feeble at best, but to testify to the greatness of the power and faithfulness of God, who has loved us and given Himself for us. There are kind friends who have graciously remarked about the work and the faith employed on the west coast. But that faith has been most imperfect. Had real faith been employed, far greater things would have been accomplished. For a movement to feel that it has faith is poor business. No group has faith as it ought to have. But even though the faith employed has been weak and imperfect, still the faithfulness of God remains, unchangeable, loving, and kind. "Even though we believe not, yet He abideth faithful" (2 Tim. 2:13 KJV).

Sometimes a man may feel that he cannot know the will of God in a certain venture. He cannot show an active faith, as far as forward movement is concerned, but he can show another type of faith, which is known as trust. He cannot see where to move, or how to act in this matter, but he can trust God to reveal Himself in plenty of time to make the move. In other words, he simply tells the Lord that he knows He will move in ample time. He does not cross his creeks until his feet are in the water. The fool may feel a thousand flames, where the trusting man scarce feels the one.

PROVISION

T HE FOLLOWING WAS written by Percy sometime in the 1970s; it is otherwise undated. It is included as his testimony, if you will, of God's meeting him and others at their points of need.

In the fifty-three years that it has been my privilege to be a humble backwoods-missionary, I have found that there are three separate and distinct facets of the care of the servant's Master. First of all is His wonderful provision for the men and women who serve both faithfully and well. Then there is the protective screen which He places around his workers, not only during working hours, but continuously, day and night. There are Scriptures aplenty to substantiate such an assertion. But lastly, the thing that makes the whole program of missions acceptable is the glorious procreation which the Holy Spirit accomplishes in and through His workers. The newborn infants of the Master's fold; the sheaves for His harvest.

To my great delight, I have found that the provision of God is a matter of great concern with God. He is more willing to give than we are to receive. He delights to give good gifts unto His children. "Ye have not because ye ask not." "Hitherto ye have asked nothing in My name," etc.

It is not the size of the need as we judge size. The need of a widow with her little brood is as important to God as is the need of a nation. The need of a sparrow is the object of His attention as much as the need of a king. You know that these things are in the Word of God, and perhaps you have tested them for your benefit before. There are no big and little things with God, just things. He said that He would supply all our need . . .

It is a matter of utmost importance for us to realize that no one has the inside track with God. He has no "teacher's pets." He has no favorites. He only recognizes the person who has faith in Himself during a time of need or distress. The word "need" is in the singular, which would indicate that we have one long need of Him from the cradle to the grave—a total and continuous need. Waking and sleeping, we need Him. Going out and coming in, we need Him. And He loves it.

So, we have the promises of God, and it behooves us to believe His Word. It is essential that we do not take hold of a promise and then let go. We need to hold on, no matter what the pressures of life may be.

One of our older workers used to say, "Remember three things when you ask God for help. First, take hold! Then, hold on! Lastly, don't let go!" It is foolish to take hold and then let go because we do not see the answer granted right away.

We so often talk about the big things and the little things which we have besought God for. But the deliverance of God for some of the so-called little things is more delightful than the so-called bigger things.

For instance, in the city of Edmonton on one trip, I was broke. I had not had a meal all day, and night was coming on. I would not beg and I would not hint to Christians that I was destitute. But I did say to the Lord, "Father, I would like something to eat, if you don't mind." I was crossing the street, and there in the streetcar tracks was a coin. Hastily I picked it up, and right in front of me was a sign in the restaurant window stating that they have waffles and coffee for the exact amount of the coin. I do not need to tell you how brief a space of time was needed to enter and eat.

Now, that is just one of a thousand "little things" which furnish the later years with constant delightful memories. Much more, oftentimes, than the bigger things of later years.

In my first charge as a missionary pastor of a little group of schoolhouses, I was very often in need of immediate and urgent deliverance. The winter had set on apace and the weather rapidly worsened. To hike the long miles to get around the parish was impossible. Time would not permit, and neither would the strength of my limbs. So I asked God for a horse, and I was given a little Indian pony which was hardly bigger than myself, but she did a marvelous job of getting me around in jig time. But there was no saddle. One day a rancher said, "Where's your saddle?" I had to admit there was no saddle in my possession. He went into his locker room and brought out a work-worn thing that certainly was no beauty, but it did save me some measure of soreness on the longer rides.

I have never known what it is to have a guaranteed income. It has been a life of total dependence on the goodness and mercy of God, and has never failed us. Of course, we have known poverty and hunger at times, but we have thanked God, as though we were honored to enter into the sufferings of Christ, in an intimate way.

It is difficult for me to understand why some workers say, "The Lord has never let me go hungry." But I do notice that they usually know where to go just before mealtime, and they usually have hearty appetites. The apostle Paul knew all about hardships and hunger, as he tells us in his great book to the Corinthians.

Besides this, most "miracles" follow the times of the most rigorous conditions, and not when the body is full of eating and sleeping. After the heartaches of life come the grace and mercy of God to the believing soul.

We were to speak in a city on the highway following a period of work in the bush near Port Alberni. As I was making the last visits among the homes of the backwoods there, and as I was preparing to pack my things and go city-wards, I asked the lady of the house if she would like to go to church the following morning. She broke into tears and said, "I have not been able to go to church for years. My husband and my sons don't let me." I was able to prevail on the men folks to release the woman from her duties the next morning, and all through the church service, in spite of my poor preaching, she quietly wept in the front pew in the auditorium. When I took her back to her home, she was radiant with a quiet joy, having fed on the Word of God for another season. That was a miracle, indeed.

It is not long before Christian workers are challenged with a stubborn fact, and that is that it is not the faith of the workers but the faithfulness of God that brings the great results. Also, that their own efforts alone are not enough to accomplish the desired results. It takes the backing of hundreds of prayers, hundreds of helpers to finish a job.

It does not leave a man with much to glory in on his own behalf. But it is a source of never-ending delight to know that the Lord on whom he depends is not only sufficient, but He is also willing to aid in any project or any need.

Personally, I have found to my dismay that even my prayers were oftentimes filled with selfish wishes or motivated by mean and despicable desires. Then, even my prayers depend on the Holy Spirit to correct the suppliant as well as the supplication, until both are brought into line with the will and purpose of God.

One of the great Scripture portions that used to be a bit of a conundrum to me was the words of the Master when He said in

Matthew's Gospel (6:22, 23 KJV), "If thine eye be single . . . and if thine eye be evil." Now, everyone knows that there is a connection between good and evil and single and double, but what connection is there between single and evil? I wondered about that for a few years until one day, one precious day, when I was to speak in a certain church on Sunday morning. I did not have the least idea what I should speak on until I came to the steps leading up to the auditorium. There I was met by a man who had a "cock-eye," as we used to call this defect. One eye tracked all right, but the other wandered around and around. He had a great deal of trouble and distress, which the doctors had been unable to correct.

Of a sudden, the Scripture portion to which I have just referred flashed into my mind, and I preached on it with great delight to my own heart. I do not know whether the folks got anything or not. There it was. Christians have one eye accepting God as the Savior of their souls, the forgiveness of sins, and life everlasting. But the other eye is roving all over the place, taking in the problems and lusts of life to their own undoing. It is the right and the duty of the Christian believer to take hold of the roving eye and bring it in line with the other and have a single vision, which is of such great delight to himself and to those who are watching from the sidelines. But when he has the second eye concentrating on his trouble and trials, his faith is insecure and his whole being is full of darkness, where there should be light. Jesus Christ should not only be the Savior of our souls, but also the Savior of our daily life with its problems and distress.

Indeed, it is this same lesson which Jesus taught His disciples in the parable of the sower. The story was given to the crowd, and when He was finished and the crowd dispersed, the disciples said, "What did you mean by that story?" To this Jesus replied that it was for their sakes and not for the crowd. Coming to the third group of seeds He said, "And the cares of this life, the deceitfulness of riches, and the lust of other things choke the Word and it becometh unfruitful" (Mk. 4:19 KJV). God grant us the ability to control the wandering eye so that we may have the fullness of joy in a life of victory with Him.

Another lesson that the Holy Spirit teaches the believer is that of the great variety of ways and means the Lord uses to get His provision to us. I always say that He can deliver by cash or by kind. Never does He use the same means a second time. Always it is new and perfectly fresh. You cannot review your life with Christ and find two deliverances with the same details, as far as relief was concerned. And no two men can ever find similar experiences in their time of comparisons. As there are no blades of grass alike, and no two snowflakes, neither are there two experiences exactly alike.

We are tempted to feel in a case of need that the man who was used of God to relieve our distress in 1970 will also be the man used of God to relieve us in 1975. So we go to visit him and, although we would never think of asking him outright, or even hint at such a thing, yet maybe he'll get the idea and slip us a buck or two. But Mr. Jones is so very busy he can't even see us, and we are tempted to run away sorrowful, with a disappointment which is keen and vivid.

Just when we think the Lord is hard on us, and should be more careful, He slips up behind us and puts the supply in our hands in a new and living way. Praise God for a living God and for a living Way.

Letters of Appreciation

FTER PERCY'S DEATH, I wrote to several people who knew him to inform them of his passing and also to ask for their recollections. Some people said that I should write a book about him, so I collected the responses I received and kept them until such time as I might write this book. At that time, the task seemed daunting.

I did not know it would take 18 years before I was asked a second time to prepare this manuscript. God knew I would need help from others who knew Percy and worked with him, and that did not happen until I moved to Lynden, Washington, where I was closer to those friends.

Among the letters I received in 1990 were a few I would like to include here. This one is from Walter Peterson, dated Armistice Day, 1990. The salutation is simply, "Percy."

It was a damp dark night in January 1943 that Milt Bryans and I knocked on the door of the big brown house on the corner of Belmont Ave. Percy Wills, the genial host of the SACA, greeted us like dear expected friends. I knew Percy for less than a year, but his life left a lasting impression on me. Physically he was not large, but his spiritual radiance melted all who came near him. He was a diplomat, optimist, humorist and a great lover. His brown eyes sparkled and danced with the excitement for life, confident that just around the corner another of God's happy surprises waited.

His deep spiritual commitment transcended all denominational boundaries—equally at ease praying with Pentecostal or Presbyterian so long as they shared his love for the Savior.

Intensely patriotic, he listened carefully on his four-tube radio to the Allies advance up the coast of Italy and plotted their position on a map. He knew how to "redeem the time." Once he came along to a little talk I gave at a Christian nurses group. During it he relaxed and (wisely) had a nap! Later he apologized—but he really shouldn't have. He acted well!

Percy bubbled with encouragement, "Don't you think I have the dearest, sweetest wife you ever saw, Walter?" giving Margarette a love pat and kiss. Once on a visit to a struggling couple in Christian work, he handed the wife a box of chocolates, saying, "Walter thought you might like these." My foot, Percy! You know very well it was all your idea, and you even bought the candy.

Sunday evenings were special at the Wills's home. A gang of young people jammed into the house to sing and share what God had done for them. It was a mixed happy group; Army, Navy and Air Force mingled with the civilians. Immersed dispersed among the unimmersed, seekers among the would-be-sought.

In spite of the heavy traffic of servicemen, the Wills had a close-knit family relationship. I have fond memories of sharing a quiet cup of tea with Margarette in the kitchen. She provided a stable, unruffled atmosphere of grace and patience in the midst of the bedlam which often prevailed. Their Jeanie was the perfect kid-sister to all of us. Her bright happy personality, her carefree attitude, her love of funny little stories all combined to make her the perfect image of our little sister back home.

We kept in contact by Christmas greetings each year. After 47 years, I had hoped to see him this summer when on a trip to Portland. Our plans were altered, so I phoned him in September with my regrets. He was alert, bright and cheerful as ever. "I still hope to see you before we get to heaven," I said. He came back, "Christians never say 'goodbye' for the last time." A great thought from a truly great man!

—Walter Peterson, Armistice day, 1990

The next letter came from Blackpool, England. It was dated June 28, 1985, and sent to the 2024 Belmont Avenue address. That date was almost 20 years after we had moved. The envelope bore the notice, "Please Forward if Necessary," and the Post Office had stamped it, "Moved, address unknown." So the writer next wrote an accompanying letter to the *Times-Colonist* newspaper, enclosing his original letter. My uncle Archie Wills had been the managing editor there when he retired, and so through that avenue Percy finally got the letter.

Dear Sir or Madam,

This may come as quite a surprise to you, but I felt I had to write to you. I'll explain!

In 1943/44 I was in the Royal Navy and was in Victoria, B.C., to collect a Landing Craft for delivery to the U.K.—on which I became part of the ship's company.

I was given a Book of the New Testament from the Christian Ass'n. of 2024 Belmont Ave., Victoria, and the name at the bottom was Mr. Percy E. Wills.

I would like you all to know that this book went with me thro' the rest of the war and it is one of my most treasured possessions and is kept permanently by my bedside here in England.

It reminds me of the kindness I, and the rest of the crew, received from all the people of Victoria whom we were fortunate enough to come into contact with . . .

I just want the brothers and sisters of the Christian Association to know that their efforts have been well appreciated by many of the crew.

—James Scorbie (ex-R.N.)

Another response to my letter informing Percy's friends of his passing came from Mr. Phillip Keller, who wrote *Splendour From The Sea*. In it, he wrote, "After the early death of my own father at 54, your father became very much a surrogate 'father' to me—virtually a fine spiritual mentor. For this I have been humbly grateful to him and even more thankful to Our Father who arranged it all."

Mr. Dick York of Shield of Faith Mission International also wrote to me. Here is a portion from his letter:

Since about 1955, when I first met your father in Ceepeecee, B.C., he has had a tremendous influence in my Christian walk. At our very first missions conference, which was Memorial Day of 1961, brother Percy was our speaker. We were so challenged by him. It was he who made me welcome the thought of growing old. He called himself "nothing but a bowlegged backwoodsman" at one of our later conferences. But as I watched him and heard him, I realized he had things that were not the result of his being bowlegged or a backwoodsman, or even an articulate student of God's Word. He had things that proceeded from the presence of God. I realized with that relationship with the Lord, greater grace was added as the years spent in God's presence multiplied.

It was your father who taught me there are no great names in the kingdom of heaven except the name of Jesus, and that our aspirations should be to be like Him, and not to seek greatness in our own right.

This next letter was written by the wife of Chief Charles Jones, Jr. of the Pacheenaht Band of First Nations people in Port Renfrew, B.C.:

> I met your father when he was here for [a] funeral, at which time he presented a Bible to our Pacheenaht Band—this was in 1976 and there were other occasions when he ministered to the Band—when a minister was needed, his was always the first name mentioned, and I have heard he did a lot of *good* work here in his early days, too. His was a much-respected name among our people. When my father-in-law, Chief Charlie Jones, Sr., went home last February, we thought of your father right away for the funeral service, but the weather was so bad we felt it would be asking too much of him at his age to make the trip in, but he did take part in the prayer service in Victoria the evening before the funeral service here. I wrote to thank him and have a treasured letter I received in reply.
>
> —Roberta O. Jones

I would like to include part of a letter Percy wrote to me after my husband died in 1975. I had moved to another city and brought my father-in-law to live with me, as he had no other children. Percy and Vera came to spend Christmas with us in our new home. I think he wanted to see what I had gotten myself into, since I had taken on a mortgage on my own signature. Previous to this time, a single woman could not obtain a loan without a co-signer, but then the law changed and I benefited from it. This letter illustrates his caring oversight of both my financial and spiritual situation. He was the same with everyone in his and Vera's families. He writes:

> How we wish we could liquidate my holdings and help each of you, but it is not possible at present.
>
> Even if we could, I do think it would not be for the good of you all, especially in your faith in God. He is teaching each

one of you, as He has taught us before you, that He alone is our source of supply, and He is not a miser. He loves to give good gifts to His children, according to His Word. And He will not forsake nor leave any of you en route to His final position for you. Your faith now will be increased and become more simple and childlike. It is in our weakness that His strength is made perfect. Read 2 Cor. 3:5.

So Vera and I pray for you daily that your faith may not fail, and that it might increase to His glory, and to your ability to strengthen others along the way. It is faith in God which we will need in the near future, and much of it. (Even more true in 2009! DJB.)

I love you very much, dear Jean, but your heavenly Father is going to become more to you than a natural father ever could be. It is impossible for me or any man or woman to teach you the deep spiritual lessons. These are in the hands of the Lord Himself, and He will allow no one to intrude in that area of your life. The Spirit Himself will instruct you in such a way that you will not only be taught, but you will learn the lessons in such a way that you could not forget them if you would.

I can well understand, my sweet, that the step you have taken is a bit scary at times. We have been through many such scary places, but each one of them became a vision of the nearness and greatness of Almighty God. We would never know how near and how great He is if He did not allow us to get into deep water at times. The greater the problems, the greater our God when He has delivered us. You are going to fall in love with God and His Son in a way you never visualized before. You will realize that He has become "a Father to the fatherless, and a real, literal husband to the widows."

May I give you a little word from my own experience, and one which became a basic rule in my missionary life? Whenever I felt butterflies and caterpillars crawling in my stomach, I breathed up a quick prayer, "Father, give me peace here. Thank You." He never fails to give peace in heart and mind when I remember, but when I am foolish He lets me sweat until I do remember, and do breathe such words.

Affectionately in Christ,
Vera and Percy

This letter was of great comfort to me at a very difficult time, and I have kept it for these many years. I have often referred to it during other times of stress. I believe his advice is timeless.

ENDNOTES

Chapter One

1. W. Phillip Keller, *Splendour from the Sea: The Saga of the Shantymen* (Chicago: Moody, 1963), p. 27.

Chapter Three

1. Denise Titian, "Truth and Reconciliation—Church Leaders Apologize to Former Residential School Students," *Ha-Shilth-Sa* (the First Nations newspaper), vol. 35, no. 5, March 13, 2008.

Chapter Four

1. W. Phillip Keller, *Splendour from the Sea: The Saga of the Shantymen* (Chicago: Moody, 1963), pp. 37-38.
2. Ibid., p. 39,40.
3. Percy E. Wills, "Intruder", *Decision* magazine (June 1976).

Chapter Five

1. Dan Dunaway, "The Shantymen – humble beginnings of a west coast ministry," *Christian Info* magazine, undated.

Chapter Six

1. Percy E. Wills, "Intruder," *Decision* magazine (June 1976).

Chapter Seven

1. W. Phillip Keller, *Splendour from the Sea: The Saga of the Shantymen* (Chicago: Moody, 1963), p. 81.

Chapter Eight

1. W. Phillip Keller, *Splendour from the Sea: The Saga of the Shantymen* (Chicago: Moody, 1963), p. 96.
2. Ibid., p. 98.
3. Louise Johnson, *Not Without Hope* (Matsqui, B.C: Maple Lane Publishing, 1992), p. 24.
4. Ibid., pp. 24, 26.
5. Ibid., p. 31, 32.
6. Ibid., pp. 55-58.
7. Ibid., pp. 133-134.

Chapter Eleven

1. Louise Johnson, *Not Without Hope* (Matsqui, B.C: Maple Lane Publishing, 1992), p. 113.
2. Ibid., p. 114.

Chapter Thirteen

1. W. Phillip Keller, *Splendour from the Sea: The Saga of the Shantymen* (Chicago: Moody, 1963), pp. 134-135.

Chapter Fourteen

1. The pertinent details of this section on the Coastal Missions Society were provided by Roy Getman. For additional information, visit the society's website at www.coastalmissions.ca.

LaVergne, TN USA
16 May 2010
182865LV00004B/25/P